STUDENT WORKBOOK

FOR

THE ART OF PUBLIC SPEAKING

Tenth Edition

Stephen E. Lucas
University of Wisconsin

Boston   Burr Ridge, IL   Dubuque, IA   Madison, WI   New York   San Francisco   St. Louis
Bangkok   Bogotá   Caracas   Kuala Lumpur   Lisbon   London   Madrid   Mexico City
Milan   Montreal   New Delhi   Santiago   Seoul   Singapore   Sydney   Taipei   Toronto

McGraw-Hill Higher Education

Student Workbook to accompany
THE ART OF PUBLIC SPEAKING
Stephen E. Lucas

Published by McGraw-Hill, an imprint of The McGraw-Hill Companies, Inc., 1221 Avenue of the Americas, New York, NY 10020. Copyright © 2009, 2007, 2004, 2001, 1998, 1995, 1992 by Stephen E. Lucas. All rights reserved.
The contents, or parts thereof, may be reproduced in print form solely for classroom use with
THE ART OF PUBLIC SPEAKING
provided such reproductions bear copyright notice, but may not be reproduced in any other form or for any other purpose without the prior written consent of The McGraw-Hill Companies, Inc., including, but not limited to, in any network or other electronic storage or transmission, or broadcast for distance learning.

3 4 5 6 7 8 9 0 QDB/QDB 5 4 3 2 1

ISBN-13: 978-0-07-726231-0
MHID: 0-07-726231-X

www.mhhe.com

TABLE OF CONTENTS

PREFACE: A MESSAGE TO STUDENTS

Welcome to your public speaking class. Although you may have enrolled in it to fulfill a requirement, you may find—as many students do—that it turns out to be your most enjoyable class of the term. Certainly it is one of the most important courses you will take in college. The skills you learn here—how to conduct research, how to organize the ideas you find in your research, how to support those ideas with evidence and reasoning, how to express yourself clearly and convincingly—will help you write term papers, make oral presentations, and compose essay exams in your other classes.

Those skills will also be invaluable in almost any career you choose. Whether you go into business, law, medicine, education, government, engineering, or community service, you will find that it is almost impossible to get ahead without strong communication skills. This is why many college graduates, in survey after survey, rank public speaking as the single most useful class of their college education. Students who enter the business world without strong public speaking skills often have to attend expensive seminars and workshops to acquire the skills they did not get in college. Your public speaking class teaches the same skills as these seminars and workshops—but at a fraction of the cost. You owe it to yourself to take full advantage of the class and the many benefits it can provide you.

Of course, none of these benefits can be acquired without work. Although many students enter their speech class thinking that it will be easy, they quickly discover that it requires a great deal of time and effort. As with most college courses, the more you put into your public speaking class, the more you will get out of it. Your instructor cannot make you become a better speaker. For that to happen, you must commit yourself to the course and be an active participant in it.

This workbook is designed to help you get the most out of your course. Written for use with your textbook, *The Art of Public Speaking*, it contains exercises, checklists, worksheets, and other materials that will help you master the principles of effective speechmaking presented in the book. At the end of the workbook, you will find evaluation forms that you can use when listening to the speeches of other students in class.

It is my hope that you will find your speech class to be a rewarding and enjoyable experience, and that this workbook will prove to be a valuable companion as you progress through *The Art of Public Speaking*.

Stephen E. Lucas
University of Wisconsin

ACKNOWLEDGMENTS

Page 5: "Student Responsibilities" is adapted, with permission of Karen P. Slawter, from course materials for Speech 101, Principles of Speech Communication, Northern Kentucky University.

Page 6: "Tips for Dealing with Speech Anxiety" is adapted, with permission of Vicki Abney Ragsdale, from course materials for Speech 101, Principles of Speech Communication, Northern Kentucky University.

Page 7: "Personal Report of Communication Apprehension (PRCA-24)" is reprinted with permission of James C. McCroskey.

Page 47: "Tips for Speaking from a Manuscript" is adapted from James A. Humes, *Talk Your Way to the Top* (New York: McGraw-Hill, 1980).

Pages 51-52: "Informative Speech Preparation Worksheet" is adapted, with permission of Kathy Kiser and Joyce Kuhn, from course materials for Speech and Drama 100, Fundamentals of Speech, Longview Community College.

HOW TO SUCCEED IN YOUR PUBLIC SPEAKING CLA

1. **Strive for Perfect Attendance.** Every session of your speech class is designed to he material and master the skills of public speaking. Some days will be devoted to lect class discussion or activities, still others to the presentation of speeches by you and you You will learn something important every day—including the days on which you are your classmates' speeches. The more faithfully you attend class, the better you will do in t

2. **Do the Assigned Readings and Do Them Ahead of Time.** Your textbook and other materials are designed to familiarize you with the principles of effective speechmaking. Wh read the assigned material ahead of time, class discussion helps reinforce your understanding of you have read in a way that doing the reading after class (or just before the exam) cannot.

3. **Learn the Language of Public Speaking.** Every area of study has its own specialized languag Terms such as *central idea*, *specific purpose*, *extemporaneous delivery*, *preparation outline*, and th like are part of the language of public speaking. Be sure you know what these terms mean.

4. **Participate in Class.** In addition to helping you learn the material better, class participation gives you additional experience expressing your ideas in front of others. Most speech classes meet in small sections in which there is ample opportunity for discussion and sharing ideas. You owe it to yourself to take advantage of this opportunity.

5. **Ask Questions.** If you have no questions about the textbook, your speeches, or the class in general, you probably aren't putting much thought into the course. Asking questions is a good way to increase your understanding of the book, to help get ready for speeches, and to feel comfortable with your instructor and classmates.

6. **Spend Lots of Time Working on Your Speeches.** To get a sense of the time commitment required for this class, think of each major speech assignment as the equivalent of writing a paper in a composition class. The process of preparing a speech includes choosing a topic, narrowing the topic and settling on a specific purpose, researching the topic, determining the main points you will develop in the speech, writing an outline of the speech and organizing it so your ideas will come across clearly and convincingly, preparing visual aids to accompany the speech, and rehearsing the speech so you can deliver it fluently and confidently. Doing all of this well requires a great deal of effort. The more time you spend working on your speeches, the better they will be. Many B speeches could become As with a little more work.

7. **Begin Working on Your Speeches Well in Advance.** Because it takes a lot of time to prepare an effective speech, it is vital that you begin working on your speeches as soon as they are assigned. This way you will be able to spend the night before your presentation fine-tuning your delivery rather than racing feverishly to prepare the content of your remarks. In addition to giving you plenty of time to work through all the stages of speech preparation, getting an early start will help you avoid the dangers of plagiarism that arise when students leave all of their speech preparation to the last minute.

8. **Get Feedback on Your Speeches.** Get feedback from your teacher. Most instructors are willing to look at several drafts of a speech and to make suggestions for improvement. You can also get feedback from family, friends, roommates, and classmates. They may not be able to give as much advice as your instructor, but they can tell you if you are saying "um" or looking down at your notes too often. Whatever you do, take advantage of feedback that can help you become a better, more confident speaker.

STUDENT INTRODUCTION QUESTIONNAIRE

Name _____ Year in School _____

Major _____

Are you taking this class as a requirement or an elective? If you are taking it to fulfill a requirement, what requirement is it fulfilling?

What kinds of speaking experiences have you had in classes, jobs, extracurricular activities, organizations, etc.?

What are your career plans? Will public speaking be important to your career? How so?

What do you believe are your greatest strengths as a public speaker? Be specific.

What are your goals for improving your public speaking in this course? Be specific.

SPEAKING WITH CONFIDENCE CHECKLIST

		Yes	No
1.	Am I enthusiastic about my speech topic?	☐	☐
2.	Have I thoroughly developed the content of my speech?	☐	☐
3.	Have I worked on the introduction so my speech will get off to a good start?	☐	☐
4.	Have I worked on the conclusion so my speech will end on a strong note?	☐	☐
5.	Have I researched my speech orally until I am confident about its delivery?	☐	☐
6.	Have I worked on turning negative thoughts about my speech into positive ones?	☐	☐
7.	Do I realize that nervousness is normal, even among experienced speakers?	☐	☐
8.	Do I understand that most nervousness is not visible to the audience?	☐	☐
9.	Am I focused on communicating with my audience, rather than on worrying about my nerves?	☐	☐
10.	Have I visualized myself speaking confidently and getting a positive response from the audience?	☐	☐

CRITERIA USED FOR EVALUATING SPEECHES

The *average speech* (grade C) should meet the following criteria:

1. Conform to the kind of speech assigned (informative, persuasive, etc.)
2. Be ready for presentation on the assigned date
3. Conform to the time limit
4. Fulfill any special requirements of the assignment such as preparing an outline, using visual aids, conducting an interview, etc.
5. Have a clear specific purpose and central idea
6. Have an identifiable introduction, body, and conclusion
7. Show reasonable directness and competence in delivery
8. Be free of serious errors in grammar, pronunciation, and word usage

The *above average speech* (grade B) should meet the preceding criteria and also:

1. Deal with a challenging topic
2. Fulfill all major functions of a speech introduction and conclusion
3. Display clear organization of main points and supporting materials
4. Support main points with evidence that meets the tests of accuracy, relevance, objectivity, and sufficiency
5. Exhibit proficient use of connectives—transitions, internal previews, internal summaries, and signposts
6. Be delivered skillfully enough so as not to distract attention from the speaker's message

The *superior speech* (grade A) should meet all the preceding criteria and also:

1. Constitute a genuine contribution by the speaker to the knowledge or beliefs of the audience
2. Sustain positive interest, feeling, and/or commitment among the audience
3. Contain elements of vividness and special interest in the use of language
4. Be delivered in a fluent, polished manner that strengthens the impact of the speaker's message

The *below average speech* (grade D or F) is seriously deficient in the criteria required for the C speech.

STUDENT RESPONSIBILITIES

1. Arrive on time for class. Arriving late is distracting and disruptive.

2. If you arrive late during a speech, do not enter the classroom. Wait by the door and enter only after you hear applause at the end of the speech.

3. Listen attentively to the speeches of your classmates. Do not read the newspaper, talk with other students, or stare out the window during a speech. Show your classmates the same courtesy and attention you expect from them when you are speaking.

4. Put away all items such as cell phones, iPods, homework, magazines, textbooks, etc. when speeches are in progress.

5. Refrain from asking questions until the end of a speech.

6. Turn in speech outlines and all other written work on the day it is due. Do not assume that late work will be accepted.

7. If you must miss a class, it is your responsibility to get all handouts, notes, and assignments from that day.

8. Be in class without fail on days when you are assigned to speak. Being absent will throw off the speaking schedule and may well result in a major penalty on your grade.

9. If you become ill and will have to miss several classes, notify your instructor immediately. Be prepared to document your illness.

10. If you cannot meet with your instructor during posted office hours, make—and keep—an appointment to meet with her or him at another time.

TIPS FOR DEALING WITH SPEECH ANXIETY

As your textbook explains, most people are nervous when faced with the prospect of giving a speech. Your aim is not to get rid of your nerves, but to manage them so they will work for you rather than against you. Learning to do so takes practice—just as it takes practice to improve other aspects of speechmaking. You can begin by following the suggestions for dealing with nervousness explained on pages 10-15 of your textbook. In addition, try the tips listed below. Over the years, many students have found them to be extremely helpful.

1. Get to know the people in your class and find out how they feel about giving speeches. Many students report—especially at the beginning of the term—that when they arise to speak, they look up from their notes to see "all those eyes on me." Get to know "those eyes." When you do, you will find that behind them are people who are just as nervous as you are.

2. Don't worry that people in the audience will see your nervousness. In most cases, students who are certain the audience can see their shaky hands and legs are told by their classmates, "Gee, I thought you looked really calm!" Remember that you are much more aware of your nervousness than are other people. If by chance your nerves do show, you will find your classmates to be extra supportive rather than extra critical.

3. Be prepared. Some students put off working on their speeches because they are nervous about the prospect of speaking. Unfortunately, waiting until the last minute to work on a speech only increases your tension and will result in a lower grade as well. Give yourself a chance to succeed. Take time to prepare your speeches well in advance.

4. Don't get flustered by the faces of audience members as you speak. Although public speakers need to be alert to audience feedback, it's important for beginning speakers to know that, despite your best efforts, some listeners will look interested and some will not. Those who do not look interested may be tired, may be worrying about their own speech, or may just have bad listening habits. Don't let them throw you off track.

5. Visualize family members and friends in the audience. Pick out three chairs—one on each side of the room and one in the middle. Now visualize a supportive family member or friend in each chair. Be specific in your mental imaging. Visualize what they are wearing, how they are sitting, the positive expressions on their faces, the way they nod their heads in support of your ideas, etc. Practicing this visualization at home as you rehearse your speech will make it even more effective.

6. Don't worry that a single mistake will ruin your speech. Some students get quite upset whenever anything goes wrong while they are speaking. If their hands shake or their voice trembles, they think they are making a fool of themselves. Or if they forget what they are going to say for a single moment, they feel as if their whole speech is a disaster. But one mistake does not destroy an entire speech any more than missing one question on an exam means that you will fail the entire test. Remember that you will be graded on many aspects of your speech other than delivery—including topic selection, research, organization, supporting materials, audience adaptation, language use, and the like. If you stumble for a moment or two in your delivery, you can still do very well on the speech as a whole.

PERSONAL REPORT OF COMMUNICATION APPREHENSION
(PRCA-24)

This questionnaire is composed of 24 statements concerning feelings about communicating with other people. Please indicate the degree to which each statement applies to you by marking whether you (1) strongly agree, (2) agree, (3) are undecided, (4) disagree, or (5) strongly disagree. Work quickly; record your first reaction.

1. Generally, I am comfortable while participating in group discussions.
2. While participating in a conversation with a new acquaintance, I feel very nervous.
3. I am very relaxed when answering questions at a meeting.
4. My thoughts become confused and jumbled while I am giving a speech.
5. I am tense and nervous while participating in group discussions.
6. Ordinarily I am very calm and relaxed in conversations.
7. I am afraid to express myself at meetings.
8. I face the prospect of giving a speech with confidence.
9. I like to get involved in group discussions.
10. Ordinarily I am very tense and nervous in conversations.
11. Communicating at meetings usually makes me uncomfortable.
12. I feel relaxed while giving a speech.
13. Engaging in a group discussion with new people makes me tense and nervous.
14. I have no fear of speaking up in conversations.
15. I am very calm and relaxed when I am called upon to express an opinion at a meeting.
16. Certain parts of my body feel very tense and rigid while I am giving a speech.
17. I am calm and relaxed while participating in group discussions.
18. I'm afraid to speak up in conversations.
19. Generally, I am nervous when I have to participate in a meeting.
20. I have no fear of giving a speech.
21. I dislike participating in group discussions.
22. While conversing with a new acquaintance, I feel very relaxed.
23. Usually I am calm and relaxed while participating in meetings.
24. While giving a speech, I get so nervous that I forget facts I really know.

SCORING: The questionnaire allows you to compute one total score and four subscores. The subscores are related to communication apprehension in four common communication contexts: group discussions, interpersonal conversations, meetings, and public speaking. To compute your scores, add or subtract your answers for each item as indicated below:

Subscore Desired	Scoring Formula
Group Discussions	18 plus scores for items 1, 9, and 17; minus scores for items 5, 13, and 21
Interpersonal Conversations	18 plus scores for items 6, 14, and 22; minus scores for items 2, 10, and 18
Meetings	18 plus scores for items 3, 15, and 23; minus scores for items 7, 11, and 19
Public Speaking	18 plus scores for items 8, 12, and 20; minus scores for items 4, 16, and 24

To obtain your total score for the PRCA, add your four subscores together. Your total score should range between 24 and 120. If your score is below 24 or above 120, you have made a mistake in computing the score. Scores on each of the four communication contexts (group discussions, interpersonal conversations, meetings, and public speaking) can range from a low of 6 to a high of 30. If your score on any context is below 6 or above 30, you have made a mistake in computing the score.

The national average across the United States for the Total Score is 65.6. National averages for each of the four communication contexts are as follows: Group Discussions—15.4; Meetings—16.4; Interpersonal Conversations—14.5; Public Speaking—19.3.

SAMPLE SPEECH OF SELF-INTRODUCTION

A HEART WORN ON MY HAND

The blistering sun beats on my forehead. I grip my fingers along the red stitching of the leather softball nestled in my hand. The batter steps up to the plate and I dig the toe of my cleats further into the pitching mound. As I prepare to pitch, my focus lies on nothing but the catcher's glove. I know my next pitch will be a strike. As I throw the ball with all my strength, the batter unleashes a hard line drive right back at me. But it's all right because I catch the ball in my glove and the batter is out.

Not only has my softball glove saved me from physical harm, but it contains hidden clues to my personality, my background, and the experiences that have helped shape who I am today.

On the outside of my glove, you notice my name scribbled in black permanent marker. My name is unique and I feel this has given me the courage to be different and stand out from my peers throughout my life. Surrounding my name you notice water stains on the leather of my glove. These stains come from practicing in the rainy spring weather in Milwaukee, Wisconsin, where I attended high school.

As you try on my glove, you notice how easily it conforms to the shape of your hand. As you open and close the glove, you notice that all the individual fingers move together with ease. This reflects how important teamwork is to me. I was captain of my softball team my senior year in high school, and I know that to accomplish any major task, everyone must move in the same direction, together.

If you look closely at the seams of my glove, you can imagine all the experiences they—and I—have been through. You can see me playing catch with my dad for the first time in my backyard. You can feel the dirt from my hand after I hit a home run and the joy I experienced after being named first team all-conference. You can see my mom, dad, younger sister, and older brother always there to support me by cheering at the games.

Over time, my softball glove has changed in appearance. Not only does it reveal aspects of my personality, my background, and my experiences, but the warm tone of the leather shows my own aging and transformations as I have grown up. As the famous basketball coach John Wooden once said, "Sports do not build character, they reveal it." Through my softball glove, my character is revealed.

SAMPLE SPEECH INTRODUCING A CLASSMATE

RHYMES WITH ORANGE

Paul Madsen's first memory in life was sitting on his grandmother's lap and being fed his favorite food—an orange. Surprisingly, there are actually many similarities between Paul and his favorite food.

Much like an orange has tough skin, so does Paul, which is evident by his choice of a major hobby—playing rugby. Paul started playing rugby while he was growing up near London, England. Rugby is described by many as the roughest sport in the world, a fact Paul can attest to since he has broken two ribs, two bones in his foot, and fractured his jaw while playing the sport. But rugby's brutal nature hasn't stopped Paul from pursuing the sport to its highest level, including leading his local team to the European championship game for its age group.

But like an orange, Paul's tough skin can be misleading. Just as an orange has a softer inside, so does Paul. He is both a caring person and a humanitarian. He has done lots of charity work throughout his life, and this past summer he went to Namibia in Southern Africa and helped build schools so the local children could have a chance to be educated. Paul also helped teach some of the children English and distributed basic health products that the children had been lacking. Paul views it as an obligation to give back to those less fortunate than him because he has been so blessed in life—especially by his loving family, which includes his mother, father, and three younger brothers.

Like an orange about to be picked from the tree, Paul has absolutely no idea where he will end up. After growing up in England, he's spending his first full year away from his homeland and is just starting to adjust to American culture. So far he's enjoying his new home immensely and is very much looking forward to furthering his education here at the university. As for a profession, Paul is not sure yet what he wants to do. He thinks he would like to have a job doing some sort of charity-related work, or he might want to coach rugby back in England.

But no matter where life takes him, one thing is for sure—Paul will eat lots of oranges along the way.

TIPS FOR USING NARRATIVE

Narratives are stories that are used to convey a lesson or a to illustrate a point. They may be real or hypothetical, brief or extended. Some narratives are based on a speaker's personal experience, others on historical events, still others on myths or fables. Narratives are important to public speakers because they translate abstract concepts into personal stories with characters, plot, conflict, and resolution. When delivered effectively, such stories pull listeners into a speech and allow the speaker to convey his or her ideas with great effectiveness. In some cultures, public speeches often revolve entirely around a lengthy narrative or a series of shorter narratives.

Depending on your speech class, you may be asked to deliver a brief narrative speech early in the term. The speech may be one in which you introduce yourself to the class, or it may be one in which you introduce a classmate. In either case, you may find yourself using narrative to explain a significant aspect of your—or your classmate's—life, culture, background, or personality. For examples of such a speech, see "A Heart Worn on My Hand" and "Rhymes with Orange," the sample introductory speeches on pages 8-9 of this workbook. Also check the sample introductory speeches on pages 70-72 of the textbook.

Whether you are introducing yourself or a classmate, there are several steps you can take to use narrative effectively.

1. Make your narrative clear and easy to follow. In most cases, it should be organized chronologically. Include transitions and other markers that will let your audience know when the narrative is shifting in time or place.

2. Be certain your narrative makes sense and answers all the questions it raises. For example, in a speech about financial aid, don't leave the audience wondering what happened to a character who was concerned about getting enough money to attend college. As with any good story, your narrative should be complete and coherent.

3. Make your narrative vivid and richly textured. Notice how the speakers provide a wealth of specific details throughout "A Heart Worn on My Hand" and "Rhymes with Orange." These details bring the narrative to life and make it interesting to listeners. Try to do the same in your speeches.

4. If you are using a hypothetical narrative—one that did not really occur—be sure to tell the audience that the story is imaginary.

5. Rehearse your narrative so you can deliver it without being tied to your speaking notes. No matter how gripping a story might be in written form, it will fall flat with listeners unless it is presented with strong eye contact and in a lively, expressive voice. Speak faster here to create a sense of action, slower there to build suspense. Raise your voice at some places and lower it in others. Pause occasionally for dramatic effect. Try to tell your story as naturally and confidently as if you were relating it to a group of friends.

CHECKLIST FOR ETHICAL PUBLIC SPEAKING

	Yes	No
1. Have I examined my goals to make sure they are ethically sound?	❑	❑
a. Can I defend my goals on ethical grounds if they are questioned or challenged?	❑	❑
b. Would I want other people to know my true motives in presenting this speech?	❑	❑
2. Have I fulfilled my ethical obligation to prepare fully for the speech?	❑	❑
a. Have I done a thorough job of studying and researching the topic?	❑	❑
b. Have I prepared diligently so as not to communicate erroneous or misleading information to my listeners?	❑	❑
3. Is the speech free of plagiarism?	❑	❑
a. Can I vouch that the speech represents my own work, my own thinking, my own language?	❑	❑
b. Do I cite the sources of all quotations and paraphrases?	❑	❑
4. Am I honest in what I say in the speech?	❑	❑
a. Is the speech free of any false or deliberately deceptive statements?	❑	❑
b. Does the speech present statistics, testimony, and other kinds of evidence fairly and accurately?	❑	❑
c. Does the speech contain valid reasoning?	❑	❑
d. If the speech includes visual aids, do they present facts honestly and reliably?	❑	❑
5. Do I use the power of language ethically?	❑	❑
a. Do I avoid name-calling and other forms of abusive language?	❑	❑
b. Does my language show respect for the right of free speech and expression?	❑	❑
6. All in all, have I made a conscious effort to put ethical principles into practice in preparing my speech?	❑	❑

AVOIDING PLAGIARISM WORKSHEET

1.   What is the meaning of "plagiarism"?

2.   According to your textbook, what is global plagiarism? Give an example.

3.   According to your textbook, what is patchwork plagiarism? Give an example.

4.   According to your textbook, what is incremental plagiarism? Give an example.

5.   What does it mean to paraphrase? How is paraphrasing similar to and different from quoting verbatim?

6.   List three guidelines from your textbook that can help you avoid plagiarism.

LISTENING SELF-EVALUATION WORKSHEET

How often do you indulge in the following 10 bad listening habits? Check yourself carefully on each one:

HABIT	FREQUENCY					SCORE
	Almost always	Usually	Some-times	Seldom	Almost never	
1. Giving in to mental distractions	____	____	____	____	____	____
2. Giving in to physical distractions	____	____	____	____	____	____
3. Trying to recall every-thing a speaker says	____	____	____	____	____	____
4. Rejecting a topic as uninteresting before hearing the speaker	____	____	____	____	____	____
5. Faking paying attention	____	____	____	____	____	____
6. Jumping to con-clusions about a speaker's meaning	____	____	____	____	____	____
7. Deciding a speaker is wrong before hearing everything she or he has to say	____	____	____	____	____	____
8. Judging a speaker on personal appearance	____	____	____	____	____	____
9. Not paying attention to a speaker's evidence	____	____	____	____	____	____
10. Focusing on delivery rather than on what the speaker says	____	____	____	____	____	____

TOTAL ____

How to score:

For every "almost always" checked, give yourself a score of	2
For every "usually" checked, give yourself a score of	4
For every "sometimes" checked, give yourself a score of	6
For every "seldom" checked, give yourself a score of	8
For every "almost never" checked, give yourself a score of	10

Total score interpretation:

Below 70	You need lots of training in listening.
From 71-90	You listen well.
Above 90	You listen exceptionally well.

SPEECH LISTENING WORKSHEET

Practice your listening skills by completing this form as you listen to a speech.

1.   What is the topic of the speech?

2.   What is the speaker's specific purpose?

3.   Which of the following methods of gaining interest and attention does the speaker use in the introduction?

☐ Relate the topic to the audience   ☐ State the importance of the topic
☐ Startle the audience   ☐ Arouse the curiosity of the audience
☐ Question the audience   ☐ Begin with a quotation
☐ Tell a story   ☐ Refer to the occasion
☐ Invite audience participation   ☐ Use visual or audio aids
☐ Refer to a previous speaker   ☐ Begin with humor

4.   Does the speaker preview the main points of the speech in the introduction?

5.   List the main points developed in the body of the speech.

6.   What pattern of organization does the speaker use?

7.   Are the speaker's main points clear and easy to follow? Why or why not?

8.   Does the speaker use a transition or other connective between each main point of the speech?

9.   Which of the following methods of referring to the central idea does the speaker use in the conclusion?

☐ Restate the main points   ☐ End with a quotation
☐ Make a dramatic statement   ☐ Refer to the introduction
☐ Challenge the audience   ☐ Call for action

CLUSTERING WORKSHEET

If you are having a difficult time coming up with a speech topic, you might try brainstorming for a topic. One method of brainstorming is clustering, which is described on pages 78-80 of your textbook. Create lists of items that come to mind under each of the following nine headings. If none of the items on your lists grabs your interest, try creating sublists for those items that seem the most promising as potential topics.

People

Places

Things

_____

_____

_____

_____

_____

_____

_____

_____

_____

_____

_____

_____

Events

Processes

Concepts

_____

_____

_____

_____

_____

_____

_____

_____

_____

_____

_____

_____

Natural Phenomena

Problems

Plans and Policies

_____

_____

_____

_____

_____

_____

_____

_____

_____

_____

_____

_____

SPECIFIC PURPOSE CHECKLIST

		Yes	No
1.	Is the specific purpose written as full infinitive phrase?	❑	❑
2.	Does the specific purpose include a reference to the audience?	❑	❑
3.	Is the specific purpose phrased as a statement rather than a question?	❑	❑
4.	Is the specific purpose free of figurative language?	❑	❑
5.	Is the specific purpose limited to a distinct subject?	❑	❑
6.	Does the specific purpose indicate precisely what I plan to accomplish in the speech?	❑	❑
7.	Does the specific purpose meet the requirements of the assignment?	❑	❑
8.	Can the specific purpose be accomplished in the time allotted for the speech?	❑	❑
9.	Is the specific purpose relevant to my audience?	❑	❑
10.	Does the specific purpose deal with a nontrivial subject?	❑	❑
11.	Is the specific purpose suitable for a nontechnical audience?	❑	❑

CENTRAL IDEA CHECKLIST

		Yes	No
1.	Is the central idea written as a complete sentence?	❑	❑
2.	Is the central idea phrased as a statement rather than a question?	❑	❑
3.	Is the central idea free of figurative language?	❑	❑
4.	Does the central idea clearly encapsulate the main points to be discussed in the body of the speech?	❑	❑
5.	Can the central idea be adequately discussed in the time allotted for the speech?	❑	❑
6.	Is the central idea relevant to the audience?	❑	❑
7.	Is the central idea appropriate for a nontechnical audience?	❑	❑

SPECIFIC PURPOSE AND CENTRAL IDEA WORKSHEET

Below are two central ideas for speeches. For each central idea provide the general purpose, specific purpose, and main points of the speech.

General Purpose:

Specific Purpose:

Central Idea: The four stages of alcoholism are the warning stage, the danger stage, the crucial stage, and the chronic stage.

Main Points:

★

General Purpose:

Specific Purpose:

Central Idea: You should join a sorority or fraternity because of the social, academic, and economic benefits.

Main Points:

PREPARING AN AUDIENCE-ANALYSIS QUESTIONNAIRE

1. Following the example on pages 109-112 of your textbook, prepare an audience-analysis questionnaire for your next speech. Design the questionnaire carefully to elicit information about the knowledge, interest, and attitudes of your classmates with regard to your speech topic. If you are giving a persuasive speech, be sure to ask about objections listeners might have to your position.

2. Your questionnaire should have a minimum of five separate questions, with seven or eight as a maximum. By all means keep the questionnaire to a single page. Be sure to use at least one of each of the three different types of questions discussed on page 110 of your textbook: fixed-alternative questions, scale questions, and open-ended questions. The more thought you put into the questionnaire, the more likely it is to be of use to you as you prepare your speech.

3. Make enough copies of your questionnaire for each member of your class. Distribute the questionnaires on the day designated by your instructor. Make sure to put your name on the questionnaire so your classmates know to whom it should be returned. Another option is to use an online tool such as Survey Monkey (www.surveymonkey.com).

4. After you have received the completed questionnaires, tabulate the results for each question, quantifying and converting results to percentages of the total audience whenever possible. When you can't quantify the results readily (as with open-ended questions), describe the results in a few sentences. Record results on a blank copy of the questionnaire.

5. After you have tabulated the results of your questionnaire, you should use those results to help adapt your speech to the knowledge, interests, and attitudes of your audience. This does not mean you should compromise your beliefs to get a favorable response. Nor does it mean you should use devious, unethical tactics to convince your listeners. You can remain true to yourself and to the principles of ethical speechmaking while simultaneously seeking to make your ideas as clear, appropriate, and convincing as possible.

6. Your instructor may ask you to write a brief paper based on the questionnaire. In this paper, you will need to state each of the questions in your questionnaire, explain why you included each question on the questionnaire, and summarize the results with respect to each question. You should also explain what the questionnaire revealed about the knowledge, interest, and attitudes of your audience with respect to the speech topic, what portion of the whole audience became the target audience for your speech, and what steps you took in the speech to adapt your ideas to the target audience.

AUDIENCE ANALYSIS WORKSHEET

Speaker _____   Topic _____

What is your audience for this speech?

What is the specific purpose of your speech?

In choosing your specific purpose, how will you narrow the topic so it will be appropriate to this audience?

Demographic audience analysis: What special adaptation is necessary in the speech because of the audience's

    age

    gender

    sexual orientation

    religion

    racial, ethnic, and cultural background

    group membership

    other (specify)

Situational audience analysis: What special adaptation is necessary in the speech because of the audience's

    size

    response to the physical setting

    knowledge about the topic

    interest in the topic

    attitude toward the topic

    disposition toward the speaker

    disposition toward the occasion

AUDIENCE ADAPTATION WORKSHEET

What device(s) will you use in the introduction to gain the attention and interest of your audience?

What steps will you take in the introduction to relate the topic directly to your audience?

What are the main points of the speech? Why do you plan to develop these particular main points for this audience?

Why have you selected the supporting materials you plan to use for this audience?

What steps have you taken to make your language clear and appropriate to this audience?

What adjustments will you make in delivery—rate of speech, volume, tone of voice, gestures, and the like—to communicate your ideas to this audience?

LIBRARY RESEARCH WORKSHEET

Name _____ Section _____

Topic: _____

Find three articles in the library on the subject of your next speech. The articles can be from periodicals or newspapers. Provide a complete citation for each article following the bibliography format required by your instructor and answer the questions about each article. (For sample bibliography formats check the online Speech Tools for Chapter 6 at connectlucas.com.)

1.   Article: _____

   _____

   Did you locate this article through a periodical database?   Yes ❑   No ❑

   If   you   answered   yes,   what   is   the   name   of   the   database?
   _____

   If you answered no, how did you locate the article? _____

   Why will the article be useful for your speech? Be specific. _____

   _____

   _____

2.   Article: _____

   _____

   Did you locate this article through a periodical database?   Yes ❑   No ❑

   If you answered yes, what is the name of the database? _____

   If you answered no, how did you locate the article? _____

   Why will the article be useful for your speech? Be specific. _____

   _____

   _____

3.   Article: _____

   _____

   Did you locate this article through a periodical database?   Yes ❑   No ❑

   If you answered yes, what is the name of the database? _____

   If you answered no, how did you locate the article? _____

   Why will the article be useful for your speech? Be specific. _____

   _____

   _____

INTERNET RESEARCH WORKSHEET

Name _____ Section _____

Topic: _____

Find two documents from the Internet on the subject of your next speech. Provide a complete citation for each article following the bibliography format required by your instructor and answer the questions about each document. (For sample bibliography formats check the online Speech Tools for Chapter 6 at connectlucas.com.)

1. Document: _____

   _____

   Did you locate this document through a search engine?   Yes ❑   No ❑

   If you answered yes, what is the name of the search engine? _____

   If you answered no, how did you locate the document? _____

   Why will the document be useful for your speech? Be specific. _____

   _____

   _____

   Explain why the author or sponsoring organization for this document should be accepted as a credible source on your speech topic.

   _____

   _____

2. Document: _____

   _____

   Did you locate this document through a search engine?   Yes ❑   No ❑

   If you answered yes, what is the name of the search engine? _____

   If you answered no, how did you locate the document? _____

   Why will the document be useful for your speech? Be specific. _____

   _____

   _____

   Explain why the author or sponsoring organization for this document should be accepted as a credible source on your speech topic.

   _____

   _____

CHECKLIST FOR EVALUATING INTERNET DOCUMENTS

	Yes	No
1. Is the author of the document clearly identified?	❑	❑
2. If the author is identified, is he or she an expert on the topic?	❑	❑
3. If the author is not an expert, can his or her opinions be accepted as objective and unbiased?	❑	❑
4. If the author is not identified, can the sponsoring organization be determined?	❑	❑
5. Is the sponsoring organization a government agency, an educational institution, or a non-profit group?	❑	❑
6. Does the sponsoring organization have a reputation for expertise and objectivity?	❑	❑
7. Does the document include a copyright date, publication date, or date of last revision?	❑	❑
8. If a date is included, is the document recent enough to cite in my speech?	❑	❑

BIBLIOGRAPHY FORMATS

	Book: Single Author
MLA	Royte, Elizabeth. *Bottlemania: How Water Went on Sale and Why We Bought It.* New York: Bloomsbury, 2008. Print.
APA	Royte, E. (2008). *Bottlemania: How water went on sale and why we bought it.* New York: Bloomsbury.
	Book: Two or More Authors
MLA	Kenney, David Ngaruri and Philip G. Schrag. *Asylum Denied: A Refugee's Struggle for Safety in America.* Berkeley: University of California Press, 2008. Print.
APA	Kenny, D.N., & Schrag, P.G. (2008). *Asylum denied: A refugee's struggle for safety in America.* Berkeley: University of California Press.
	Book: Second or Later Edition
MLA	Green, Alan P. and Alan S. Gerber. *Get Out the Vote: How to Increase Voter Turnout.* 2nd ed. Washington, D.C.: Brookings Institution Press, 2008. Print.
APA	Green, A.P., & Gerber, A.S. (2008). *Get out the vote: How to increase voter turnout.* Washington, D.C.: Brookings Institution Press.
	Book: Corporate Author
MLA	American Bar Association. *ABA Standards for Criminal Justice: DNA Evidence.* 3rd ed. Washington, D.C.: American Bar Association, 2007. Print.
APA	American Bar Association. (2007). *ABA standards for criminal justice: DNA evidence* (3rd ed.). Washington, DC: Author.
	Book: Anthology or Compilation
MLA	Olson, Alix, ed. *Word Warriors: 35 Women Leaders in the Spoken Word Revolution.* Emeryville, CA: Seal Press, 2007. Print.
APA	Olson, A. (Ed.). (2007). *Word warriors: 35 women leaders in the spoken word revolution.* Emeryville, CA: Seal Press.

Chapter in Anthology or Compilation	
MLA	Lamm, Nomy. "Book of Rules: A Girl's Guide to Doing What You're Told." *Word Warriors: 35 Women Leaders in the Spoken Word Revolution*. Ed. Alix Olson. Emeryville, CA: Seal Press, 2007. 210-212. Print.
APA	Lamm, N. (2007). Book of rules: A girl's guide to doing what you're told. In A. Olson (Ed.) *Word warriors: 35 women leaders in the spoken word revolution* (pp. 210-212). Emeryville, CA: Seal Press.
Signed Magazine Article	
MLA	Carr, Nicholas. "Is Google Making Us Stupid? What the Internet Is Doing to Our Brains." *Atlantic* July–Aug. 2008: 56-63. Print.
APA	Carr, N. (2008, July/August). Is Google making us stupid? What the internet is doing to our brains. *The Atlantic, 302*, 56-63.
Unsigned Magazine Article	
MLA	"Food and the Poor: The New Face of Hunger." *Economist* 17 Apr. 2008: 32-34. Print.
APA	Food and the poor: The new face of hunger. (2008, April 17). *The Economist, 387*, 32-34.
Journal Article, Continuous Pagination	
MLA	Stewart, Dafina Lazarus. "Being All of Me: Black Students Negotiating Multiple Identities." *Journal of Higher Education* 79.2 (2008): 183-207. Print.
APA	Stewart, D.L. (2008). Being all of me: Black students negotiating multiple identities. *The Journal of Higher Education, 79*, 183-207.
Journal Article, Noncontinuous Pagination	
MLA	Sautman, Barry and Yan Hairong. "Friends and Interests: China's Distinctive Links with Africa." *African Studies Review* 50.3 (2007): 75-114. Print.
APA	Sautman, B., & Hairong, Y. (2007). Friends and interests: China's distinctive links with Africa. *African Studies Review, 50*(3), 75-114.

Signed Newspaper Article	
MLA	Witt, Howard. "Hispanics Lead Pace in Diverse Nation." *Chicago Tribune* 1 May 2008, south-southwest ed., sec. 1: 4. Print.
APA	Witt, H. (2008, May 1). Hispanics lead pace in diverse nation. *Chicago Tribune*, section 1, p. 4.
Unsigned Newspaper Article	
MLA	"Gene Therapy Offers Promising Results for Some Blind Patients." *Star Tribune* [Minneapolis-St. Paul] 28 Apr. 2008: A4. Print.
APA	Gene therapy offers promising results for some blind patients. (2008, April 28). *Star Tribune*, p. A4.
Signed Newspaper Editorial	
MLA	Brooks, David. "The Cognitive Age." Editorial. *New York Times* 2 May 2008, natl. ed.: A23. Print.
APA	Brooks, D. (2008, May 2). The cognitive age [Editorial]. *The New York Times*, p. A23.
Unsigned Newspaper Editorial	
MLA	"To Be Young and Voting." Editorial. *Christian Science Monitor* 5 May 2008: 8. Print.
APA	To be young and voting [Editorial]. (2008, May 5). *The Christian Science Monitor*, p. 8.
Government Publication	
MLA	United States. U.S. Dept. of Labor. U.S. Bureau of Labor Statistics. *Occupational Outlook Handbook, 2008–2009 Library Edition*. Washington, D.C.: GPO, 2008. Print.
APA	U.S. Bureau of Labor Statistics. (2008). *Occupational outlook handbook, 2008–2009 library edition*. Washington, DC: U.S. Government Printing Office.

	Signed Article in Reference Work
MLA	Roppolo, Kimberly. "Sweat Lodges." *Encyclopedia of American Indian History*. Eds. Bruce E. Johansen and Barry M. Pritzker. 4 vols. Santa Barbara, CA: ABC-CLIO, 2008. Print.
APA	Roppolo, K. (2008). Sweat lodges. In B. Johansen and B. Pritzker (Eds.), *Encyclopedia of American Indian history* (Vol. 2, pp. 473-474). Santa Barbara, CA: ABC-CLIO.
	Unsigned Article in Reference Work
MLA	"Shirin Ebadi." *International Who's Who 2008*. 71st ed. London: Routledge, 2007. Print.
APA	Shirin Ebadi. (2007). In *International Who's Who 2008* (p. 601). London: Routledge.
	Personal Interview
MLA	Rodriquez, James. Personal interview. 15 Oct. 2008.
APA	J. Rodriquez (personal communication, October 15, 2008)
	Letter or E-Mail Communication
MLA	Mattson, Ingrid. Message to the author. 17 June 2008. E-mail.
APA	I. Mattson (personal communication, June 17, 2008)
	Speech or Lecture
MLA	Hassenzahl, David. "Industrialization and Climate." Environmental Studies 206: Introduction to Climate Change. University of Nevada, Las Vegas. 16 Sept. 2008. Lecture.
APA	Hassenzahl, D. (2008, September). Industrialization and climate. Lecture presented in Environmental Studies 206: Introduction to climate change. University of Nevada, Las Vegas.
	Television Program
MLA	"The Medicated Child." Narr. Will Lyman. *Frontline*. PBS. WGBH, Boston, 8 Jan. 2008. Television.
APA	Gaviria, M. (Writer and Director). (2008). The medicated child [Television series episode]. In R. Aronson-Rath (Senior Producer), *Frontline*. New York and Washington, D.C.: Public Broadcasting Service.

Film	
MLA	*Dare Not Walk Alone: A War of Responsibility*. Dir. Jeremy Dean. Indican Pictures, 2008. Film.
APA	Dean, J. (Director), & Mergener, R. (2008). *Dare not walk alone: A war of responsibility* [Motion picture]. United States. (Available from Indican Pictures, 8424A Santa Monica Boulevard #752, West Hollywood, CA 90069)
Article in Scholarly Journal Reprinted Online	
MLA	Young, Robert, Helen Sweeting, and Patrick West. "A Longitudinal Study of Alcohol Use and Antisocial Behavior in Young People." *Alcohol and Alcoholism*. 43.2 (2008): 204-214. *Oxford Journals*. Web. 5 June 2008.
APA	Young, R., Sweeting, H., & West, P. (2008). A longitudinal study of alcohol use and antisocial behavior in young people. *Alcohol and Alcoholism, 43*(2), 204-214. doi:10.1093/alcalc/agm147
Article in Online Scholarly Journal	
MLA	Rajendran, Diana, Luke A. Downey, and Con Stough. "Assessing Emotional Intelligence in the Indian Workplace: A Preliminary Reliability Study." *Electronic Journal of Applied Psychology* 3.2 (2007): 55-59. Web. 24 June 2008.
APA	Rajendran, D., Downey, L., & Stough, C. (2007). Assessing emotional intelligence in the Indian workplace: A preliminary reliability study. *Electronic Journal of Applied Psychology, 3*(2). Retrieved from http://ojs.lib.swin.edu.au/index.php/ejap/article/view/85/124
Online Government Publication	
MLA	United States. Dept. of Health and Human Services. National Institute of Mental Health. *Panic Disorder*. 2 Apr. 2008. *National Institute of Mental Health*. Web. 7 July 2008.
APA	National Institute of Mental Health (2008, April). *Panic disorder*. Retrieved from http://www.nimh.nih.gov/health/topics/index.shtml
Online Newspaper Article	
MLA	Daley, Beth. "Not As Green As They Claim To Be." *Boston Globe* 14 May 2008. *Boston.com*. Web. 5 June 2008.
APA	Daley, B. (2008, May 14). Not as green as they claim to be. *Boston Globe*. Retrieved from http://www.boston.com

Online Editorial	
MLA	Cirincione, J. "A Critical Mass for Disarmament: Change, Failure, and Fear Are Propelling Us toward a World without Nuclear Weapons." Editorial. *Los Angeles Times* 4 June 2008. *Latimes.com*. Web. 5 June 2008.
APA	Cirincione, J. (2008, June 4). A critical mass for disarmament: Change, failure, and fear are propelling us toward a world without nuclear weapons [Editorial]. *Los Angeles Times*. Retrieved from http://www.latimes.com
Online Magazine Article	
MLA	Ripley, Amanda. "How to Survive a Disaster." *Time* 29 May 2008. *Time.com*. Web. 6 June 2008.
APA	Ripley, A. (2008, May 29). How to survive a disaster. *Time*. Retrieved from http://www.time.com
Document Accessed from Online Service	
MLA	Trejos, Nancy. "Majoring in Plastic: With Easy Access to Credit Cards, Students Pick Up Debt Habit Early." *Washington Post* 13 April 2008: F01. *LexisNexis*. Web. 5 June 2008.
APA	Trejos, N. (2008, April 13). Majoring in plastic: With easy access to credit cards, students pick up debt habit early. *Washington Post*. Retrieved from LexisNexis Academic database.
Online News Source	
MLA	Cohen, Elizabeth. "Your Private Health Details May Already Be Online." *CNN.com*. Cable News Network, 5 June 2008. Web. 29 June 2008.
APA	Cohen, E. (2008, June 5). Your private health details may already be online. *Cable News Network*. Retrieved from http://www.cnn.com
Online Encyclopedia	
MLA	"Kahlo, Frida." *Encyclopaedia Britannica Online*. Encyclopedia Britannica, 2008. Web. 8 July 2008.
APA	Kahlo, Frida. (2008). In *Encyclopaedia Britannica*. Retrieved July 8, 2008, from http://www.britannica.com

CHECKLIST FOR USING EXAMPLES

		Yes	No
1.	Do I use examples to clarify my ideas?	❑	❑
2.	Do I use examples to reinforce my ideas?	❑	❑
3.	Do I use examples to personalize my ideas?	❑	❑
4.	Are my examples representative of what they are supposed to illustrate or prove?	❑	❑
5.	Do I reinforce my examples with statistics or testimony?	❑	❑
6.	Are my extended examples vivid and richly textured?	❑	❑
7.	Have I practiced the delivery of my extended examples to give them dramatic effect?	❑	❑

CHECKLIST FOR USING STATISTICS

	Yes	No
1. Do I use statistics to quantify my ideas?	❏	❏
2. Are my statistics representative of what they purport to measure?	❏	❏
3. Are my statistics from reliable sources?	❏	❏
4. Do I cite the sources of my statistics?	❏	❏
5. Do I use statistical measures (mean, median, mode) correctly?	❏	❏
6. Do I round off complicated statistics?	❏	❏
7. Do I use visual aids to clarify statistical trends?	❏	❏
8. Do I explain my statistics and relate them to the audience?	❏	❏

CHECKLIST FOR USING TESTIMONY

	Yes	No

1. Do I use testimony to support my ideas? ☐ ☐

2. Do I use testimony from qualified sources? ☐ ☐

3. Do I use testimony from unbiased sources? ☐ ☐

4. Do I distinguish between expert testimony and peer testimony? ☐ ☐

5. Do I identify the sources of all testimony? ☐ ☐

6. Do I quote and paraphrase all sources of testimony with complete accuracy? ☐ ☐

SUPPORTING MATERIALS WORKSHEET

Evaluate the use of supporting materials in the following speech excerpt. Be sure to deal with all the supporting materials in each paragraph, and be specific in assessing their strengths and weaknesses.

According to emergency medicine specialist Dr. Randall Sword, emergency rooms will handle more than 160 million cases this year alone. This means that one out of every 16 Americans will spend time in an emergency room this year. Unfortunately, the National Academy of Sciences states that "emergency medical care is one of the weakest links in the delivery of health care in the nation." In fact, medical researchers estimate that 5,000 deaths annually from poisoning, drowning, and drug overdoses, as well as 20 percent of all deaths from automobile accidents, would not have happened if the victims had received prompt and proper emergency room care.

One cause of this problem is that many doctors are not properly trained in emergency care. According to *U.S. News and World Report*, fewer than 50 percent of emergency room physicians have completed special emergency training courses. A survey by Frey and Mangold found that untrained emergency room physicians felt they were unsure how to diagnose or treat many of the extreme abdomen, chest, and cardiac disorders that often appear in hospital emergency rooms.

Another cause of the problem is that precious time is often wasted on useless paperwork before vital emergency treatment begins. Several years ago, a man driving by an elementary school in my hometown had a heart attack and crashed into a schoolyard. Seven children were taken to the emergency room three blocks away, but the real tragedy had not yet begun. Once in the emergency room, the children were denied treatment until their parents were contacted and the admitting forms were filled out. By the time the forms were completed, two of the children had died.

CHECKLIST FOR CITING SOURCES ORALLY

		Yes	No
1.	Do I identify all the print documents cited in my speech?	❑	❑
2.	Do I identify all the Web documents cited in my speech?	❑	❑
3.	Do I identify the authors or sponsoring organizations of the documents I cite?	❑	❑
4.	Do I establish the authors' credentials with regard to the topic?	❑	❑
5.	Do I use documents from sponsoring organizations with established expertise and objectivity?	❑	❑
6.	Do I include the dates on which the documents were published, posted, or updated?	❑	❑
7.	Do I use a variety of methods in citing my sources?	❑	❑

SPEECH ORGANIZATION WORKSHEET

Identify the organizational method used in each of the following sets of main points.

I.   Early people did not have money but used a system of exchange based on the barter of goods and services.
II.   Coin money was invented in ancient Turkey, China, and India before the birth of Christ.
III. Paper money began in China about 600 A.D. but did not become popular in the West until the 1600s.
IV.   Today almost every country has an official currency tied to the international rate of exchange.

★

I.   Genetic engineering is producing new plant hybrids that will vastly increase world agricultural production.
II.   Genetic engineering is producing breakthroughs in medicine that will allow people to live healthier lives.
III. Genetic engineering is producing bacteria that will help clean up industrial pollutants.

★

I.   Gambling addiction is an increasingly serious problem throughout the United States.
II.   The problem of gambling addiction can best be solved by a combination of education and rehabilitation.

★

I.   There are several causes for the destruction of the rain forests in South America.
II.   If the destruction of the rain forests continues, the effects will have global impact.

★

I.   The top layer of the earth is a rocky "skin" called the crust.
II.   Beneath the crust is a thick layer of rock called the mantle.
III. The next lower section is a mass of melted rock called the outer core.
IV.   At the center of the earth is a solid mass called the inner core.

MAIN POINTS CHECKLIST

		Yes	No
1.	Does the body of my speech contain two to five main points?	❏	❏

2. Are my main points organized according to one of the following methods of organization? (Check the one that applies.)

	Yes	No
Chronological order	❏	❏
Spatial order	❏	❏
Causal order	❏	❏
Topical order	❏	❏
Problem-Solution order	❏	❏
Problem-Cause-Solution order	❏	❏
Monroe's motivated sequence	❏	❏

		Yes	No
3.	Are my main points clearly separate from one another?	❏	❏
4.	As much as possible, have I used the same pattern of wording for all my main points?	❏	❏
5.	Have I roughly balanced the amount of time devoted to each main point?	❏	❏
6.	Is each main point backed up with strong, credible supporting materials?	❏	❏
7.	Do I use connectives to make sure my audience knows when I am moving from one main point to another?	❏	❏

CONNECTIVES WORKSHEET

As discussed on pages 177-180 of your textbook, connectives are words or phrases that connect the ideas of a speech and indicate the relationships among them. Below are excerpts from two speech outlines—one on immigration, the other on the shortage of nurses in U.S. hospitals. For each outline, provide the connective(s) indicated in the space provided.

***

I.   Over the years, millions of people have immigrated to the United States.
A. Since the American Revolution, almost 90 million people have immigrated to the U.S.
B. Today there are over 37 million Americans who were born in other countries.

Transition: _____

_____

_____

II.   There are several reasons why people immigrate to the United States.
A. Many people immigrate in search of economic opportunity.
B. Others immigrate to attain political freedom.
C. Still others immigrate to escape religious persecution.

Internal Summary: _____

_____

_____

_____

***

I.   The shortage of nurses has become a serious national problem.
A. More than 60 percent of U.S. hospitals have nurse shortages severe enough to threaten the quality of health care.
B. Experts warn that the shortage will become even worse in the years ahead unless steps are taken to solve it.

Transition and Internal Preview: _____

_____

_____

_____

II.   The problem can be solved by offering nurses better salaries and better working conditions.
A. Better salaries will attract more people to nursing as a profession.
B. Better working conditions will improve morale and reduce burnout among nurses.

SPEECH INTRODUCTION CHECKLIST

		Yes	No
1.	Do I gain the attention and interest of my audience by using one or more of the methods discussed in this chapter?	❑	❑
2.	Do I relate the speech topic to my audience?	❑	❑
3.	Do I clearly reveal the topic of my speech?	❑	❑
4.	Do I establish my credibility to speak on this topic?	❑	❑
5.	If my topic is controversial, do I take steps to establish my goodwill toward the audience?	❑	❑
6.	Do I define any key terms that will be necessary for the audience to understand the rest of my speech?	❑	❑
7.	Do I provide a preview statement of the main points to be covered in the body of the speech?	❑	❑
8.	Is the introduction limited to 10-20 percent of my entire speech?	❑	❑
9.	Have I worked out the language of my introduction in detail?	❑	❑
10.	Have I practiced the delivery of my introduction so I can present it fluently, confidently, and with strong eye contact?	❑	❑

SPEECH CONCLUSION CHECKLIST

	Yes	No
1. Do I signal that my speech is coming to an end?	☐	☐
2. Do I reinforce my central idea by (check all that apply):		
Summarizing the main points of my speech	☐	☐
Ending with a quotation	☐	☐
Making a dramatic statement	☐	☐
Referring to the introduction	☐	☐
3. Is the conclusion limited to 5-10 percent of my entire speech?	☐	☐
4. Have I worked out the language of my conclusion in detail?	☐	☐
5. Have I practiced the delivery of my conclusion so I can present it fluently, confidently, and with strong eye contact?	☐	☐

SPEECH INTRODUCTION WORKSHEET

Below are four complete introductions from classroom speeches. Each has at least one flaw that keeps it from fulfilling all the major functions of an effective introduction discussed on pages 186-197 of your textbook: (1) Gain the attention and interest of the audience; (2) Reveal the topic of the speech; (3) Establish credibility and goodwill; (4) Preview the body of the speech. In each case identify the flaw (or flaws) and make specific suggestions for improving the introduction.

1. What tiny crystal fortified the coffers of many ancient empires and laid waste to others? What mineral has the power to create and the power to destroy? What is "good as gold" when scarce and "cheap as dirt" when abundant?

    The answer to all of these questions is salt, the spice of life. Today I would like to look at the importance of salt in history, at how we spice up our lives with salt today, and at the role salt will probably play in the future.

2. We have so much unused human potential. By improving the use of your time, you can have much more time for social activities. You can use your mental processes more fully, thereby improving your grades. You can also increase your physical stamina and improve your health. We must learn to know our bodies.

3. A six-year-old collie lay battered and helpless by the side of the road. The car that hit her had broken her pelvis, dislocated her hip, and smashed her jaw. It had also blinded her, and she whimpered in pain and fear.

    Unfortunately, this true story happens much too frequently because of the growing problem of pet overpopulation. Having grown up on a farm with animals of all kinds, I care deeply about their welfare, and I have become aware through my veterinary courses of how serious the problem of pet overpopulation is.

4. Every problem has at least two sides. When one side is right, and the other side is wrong, the problem is easy to solve. But what if both sides have merit in their arguments? How do you solve these problems?

    Balancing the rights of everyone in an adoption is one of these problems. The parents who give up the child have a right that all the information they disclose be kept confidential, while the adopted child has a right to know about the identity of his or her natural parents.

    Today I'd like to explore this problem with you and look at one approach to solving it.

PREPARATION OUTLINE GUIDE

The following is a guide to use as you develop preparation outlines for your speeches. For purposes of illustration, this guide has three main points in the body of the speech. In your speeches, of course, the number and organization of main points, subpoints, and sub-subpoints will vary depending on the topic and purpose of any given speech. However, the elements needed in the outline—title, specific purpose statement, central idea, introduction, body, conclusion, connectives, bibliography—will remain the same. For more information, check the guidelines for preparation outlines and the sample preparation outline with commentary on pages 208-215 of your textbook.

Name:

Date:

Section:

TITLE

[Check with your instructor to see if you need to include a title with your outline. If you do, be sure to consult the discussion of speech titles on pages 211-213 of your textbook.]

Specific Purpose Statement: [Should fit the criteria for specific purpose statements on pages 81-87 of your textbook]

Central Idea: [Should fit the criteria for central ideas on pages 87-91 of your textbook]

INTRODUCTION

[Check with your instructor to see whether the introduction should be written out word for word or presented in outline form. In either case, label the introduction as a distinct section of the speech and make sure it fulfills all four major objectives of an introduction explained on pages 186-196 of your textbook: (1) Gain the attention and interest of the audience; (2) Reveal the topic of the speech; (3) Establish credibility and goodwill; (4) Preview the body of the speech.]

(*Connective*: Make sure the audience knows you are moving from the introduction into the first main point of the body. For information on connectives, review pages 177-180 of your textbook.)

BODY

I.   A single complete sentence expressing the main point of this section of the speech.
   A.   Subpoint [As with main points, subpoints should be written in full sentences.]
      1.   Sub-subpoint [Check with your instructor to see whether sub-subpoints need to be written as full sentences.]
      2.   Sub-subpoint
   B.   Subpoint

(*Connective*: Use a transition or other connective to help the audience move with you from one main point to the next.)

II. A single complete sentence expressing the main point of this section of the speech.
  A. Subpoint
  B. Subpoint
    1. Sub-subpoint
      a. Sub-sub-subpoint
      b. Sub-sub-subpoint
    2. Sub-subpoint

(*Connective*: Use a transition or other connective to help the audience move with you from one main point to the next.)

III. A single complete sentence expressing the main point of this section of the speech.
  A. Subpoint
    1. Sub-subpoint
    2. Sub-subpoint
  B. Subpoint
    1. Sub-subpoint
    2. Sub-subpoint
    3. Sub-subpoint
  C. Subpoint

(*Connective*: Use a transition or other connective to help the audience move with you from the body of your speech to the conclusion.)

CONCLUSION

[Check with your instructor to see whether the conclusion should be written out word for word or presented in outline form. In either case, label the conclusion as a distinct section of the speech and make sure it fulfills both major objectives of a conclusion explained on pages 197-202 of your textbook: (1) Let the audience know you are ending the speech; (2) Reinforce the audience's understanding of, or commitment to, the central idea.]

BIBLIOGRAPHY

[Here you list complete citations for the research materials used in preparing your speech. The two major bibliographic formats are those recommended by the Modern Language Association (MLA) and the American Psychological Association (APA). Sample citations for both are provided on pages 25-30 of this workbook. Check with your instructor to see which format you should use for your bibliography.]

PREPARATION OUTLINE CHECKLIST

		Yes	**No**
1.	Does my speech have a title, if one is required?	❑	❑
2.	Do I state the specific purpose before the text of the outline itself?	❑	❑
3.	Do I state the central idea before the text of the outline itself?	❑	❑
4.	Are the introduction, body, and conclusion clearly labeled?	❑	❑
5.	Are main points and subpoints written in full sentences?	❑	❑
6.	Are transitions, internal summaries, and internal previews clearly labeled?	❑	❑
7.	Does the outline follow a consistent pattern of symbolization and indentation?	❑	❑
8.	Does the outline provide a clear visual framework that shows the relationships among the ideas of my speech?	❑	❑
9.	Does the bibliography identify all the sources I consulted in preparing the outline?	❑	❑
10.	Does the bibliography follow the format required by my instructor?	❑	❑

SCRAMBLED OUTLINE WORKSHEET

In the left-hand column below is a blank outline from a speech about Booker T. Washington. In the right-hand column, arranged in random order, are the subpoints and sub-subpoints to fill in the outline. Choose the appropriate subpoint or sub-subpoint for each blank in the outline.

Outline	*Subpoints and Sub-Subpoints*
I. Booker T. Washington is best known for founding Tuskegee Institute in Alabama.	All told, Washington delivered some 4,000 public speeches during his 30-year career as an orator.
A.	Some people praise the speech as a brilliant example of audience adaptation in a very difficult situation.
1.	When Washington founded Tuskegee Institute in 1881, the school had only one dilapidated building and an enrollment of 40 students.
2.	Today, Tuskegee Institute remains a leader in applied research and practical education.
B.	Washington's most famous speech is his Atlanta Exposition Address of 1895.
II. Washington is also known as one of the best speakers in American history.	The growth of Tuskegee Institute under Washington's guidance was nothing short of phenomenal.
A.	To this day, Washington's speech at Atlanta remains highly controversial.
B.	By the time Washington died in 1915, Tuskegee Institute occupied 2,000 acres of land, enrolled 1,500 students, and boasted a faculty of 200 instructors.
1.	Other people condemn the speech for failing to denounce racial segregation and inequality.
2.	In the Atlanta Exposition Address Washington urged blacks to strive for economic advancement rather than to agitate for immediate social equality.
a.	
b.	

TIPS FOR THE SPEAKING OUTLINE

1. Keep your speaking outline as brief as possible. Reduce your speech to key words and phrases (except for direct quotations, statistics, source citations, and certain key ideas) to enhance the extemporaneous quality of your delivery.

2. Follow the visual framework of symbolization and indentation used in your preparation outline. This will make it easier for you to see where you are in the speech at any given moment.

3. Some people put their speaking outlines on index cards; others prefer to write them on paper or to print them from a computer. Either can work fine as long as your notes are immediately legible to you while you are speaking. Check with your instructor to see if she or he has any preferences in this regard.

4. Most speakers who use index cards find the 3 X 5 size too cramped and prefer the 4 X 6 or 5 X 8 sizes instead.

5. If you put your speaking outline on index cards, try to use one card for each main point, plus one card each for the introduction and conclusion. This will reinforce the distinctiveness of each point and will help you pause at appropriate moments during the speech.

6. Whether you use index cards or regular paper, write on only one side of each card or sheet of paper. Limit the amount of information on each card or sheet of paper so you can read it at a glance under the pressure of the speech situation. Number each card or sheet of paper in the upper right-hand corner so it is easy for you to make sure they are in order.

7. If you compose your speaking outline on a computer, use a large readable font. It is not a good idea to use all capital letters, since research has shown that a lot of words in ALL CAPS is harder to read than is normal text. Use generous margins and provide extra space between lines.

8. If you are composing your outline on a computer and want to use index cards for your speaking notes, format the pages on your computer to correspond with the size of your index cards. You can then print your notes on computer paper and tape or glue them to your index cards.

9. If you write your speaking outline by hand, do not use pencil, which smudges easily and is often too light to read without straining.

10. Give yourself cues for delivering the speech. Remind yourself to maintain eye contact and to gesture. Tell yourself when to pause, where to speak louder, and the like. Also include signals that will remind you when to display and remove visual aids. Use highlighters or brightly colored markers for delivery cues to make sure you will not overlook them during the speech.

11. Prepare your speaking outline far enough in advance that you will have plenty of time to practice with it as you rehearse the speech.

TIPS FOR SPEAKING FROM A MANUSCRIPT

1. Write your speech for the ear. It should be prepared with simple words, short sentences, and the rhythm of conversation. As you work on the speech, keep saying the lines out loud, listening for the rhythms of oral style. If possible, record your first draft on your computer, iPod, or other device. Listen to yourself to find the awkward phrases that need revision.

2. Make sure your manuscript is easy to read. Use wide margins and double or triple space between lines. Use a large font that can be deciphered at a glance. Do not use all capital letters, since research has shown that they are harder to read than a combination of capital letters and lower-case letters. Print the manuscript on firm paper that will not crinkle or roll up at the edges.

3. Do not recite the manuscript word for word when you deliver the speech. Instead, look down at the page, "photograph" a phrase in your mind, and deliver the phrase. Try not to speak when your eyes are fixed on the page. Talk through the text, rather than worrying about saying every word just as it is written. You are the only person who will know when the speech departs slightly from the manuscript.

4. Don't try to "photograph" too much text at a time. Let your eye record what you can remember comfortably, then look up and speak to the audience. Break sentences into oral chunks. Strive for bite-sized groups of words that are comfortable to utter in one breath.

5. Don't be afraid to pause between statements. At first, this may feel awkward, but frequent pauses are a normal part of everyday conversation and they will not seem unnatural to your audience.

6. Establish eye contact with your audience while you are speaking. Look for someone who seems to be listening intently and speak to that person. Then switch your attention to another part of the room and engage someone else's gaze. The quickest way to lose your audience is to spend the entire speech staring at your manuscript in an effort to recite every word just the way it is written.

7. Use vocal variety to give your speech impact. Your words must be given time to sink in and to register with the audience. Remember that your listeners cannot see your speech—they can only hear it.

8. Mark your speaking text to indicate places where you want to speed up, slow down, speak louder or softer, pause, and the like. There is a key word in every line. Find that word, underline it on your text, and be sure to give it proper emphasis when you speak.

9. Practice. Delivering a speech effectively from manuscript takes time and effort. In many ways, it is harder than speaking extemporaneously. The more you practice, the more likely you are to present the speech with strong eye contact and a conversational tone.

OUT-OF-CLASS SPEECH OBSERVATION WORKSHEET

Your name _____Speaker _____

Where was the speech presented? _____

What was the occasion for the speech? _____

Vocal Communication: *Record your observations about each of the following aspects of the*
speaker's voice.

Volume _____

Pitch _____

Rate _____

Pauses _____

Vocal variety _____

Pronunciation _____

Articulation _____

Physical Action: *Record your observations about each of the following aspects*
of the speaker's physical action.

Personal appearance _____

Movement _____

Gestures _____

Eye contact _____

Overall Evaluation of Delivery: *Explain how the speaker's delivery added to or*
detracted from the message.

_____

_____

_____

What It Means For Me: *Explain at least two techniques of delivery used by the speaker that*
you might want to try in your next speech.

_____

_____

CHECKLIST FOR PREPARING VISUAL AIDS

		Yes	No
1.	Have I prepared my visual aids well in advance?	☐	☐
2.	Are my visual aids clear and easy to comprehend?	☐	☐
3.	Does each visual aid contain only the information needed to make my point?	☐	☐
4.	Are my visual aids large enough to be seen clearly by the entire audience?	☐	☐
5.	Do the colors on my visual aids work well together?	☐	☐
6.	Is there a clear contrast between the lettering and background on my charts, graphs, and drawings?	☐	☐
7.	Do I use line graphs, pie graphs, and bar graphs correctly to show statistical trends and patterns?	☐	☐
8.	Do I limit charts to no more than eight items?	☐	☐
9.	Do I use fonts that are easy to read?	☐	☐
10.	Do I use a limited number of fonts?	☐	☐

CHECKLIST FOR PRESENTING VISUAL AIDS

		Yes	No
1.	Can I present my visual aids without writing or drawing on the chalkboard?	☐	☐
2.	Have I checked the speech room to decide where I can display my visual aids most effectively?	☐	☐
3.	Have I practiced presenting my visual aids so they will be clearly visible to everyone in the audience?	☐	☐
4.	Have I practiced setting up and taking down my visual aids so I can do both smoothly during the speech?	☐	☐
5.	Have I practiced keeping eye contact with my audience while presenting my visual aids?	☐	☐
6.	Have I practiced explaining my visual aids clearly and concisely in terms my audience will understand?	☐	☐
7.	If I am using handouts, have I planned to distribute them after the speech rather than during it?	☐	☐
8.	Have I double-checked all equipment to make sure it works properly?	☐	☐
9.	Have I rehearsed my speech with the equipment I will use during the final presentation?	☐	☐

INFORMATIVE SPEECH PREPARATION WORKSHEET

Name _____ Section _____

1. What is the topic of your speech? Why is it appropriate for you? _____
    _____
    _____
    _____

2. Why is the topic appropriate for your audience? _____
    _____
    _____
    _____

3. How is your topic narrowed to conform to the time limits for the speech assignment?
    _____
    _____
    _____

4. What is your specific purpose statement? _____
    _____
    _____

5. Can you answer yes to all the questions on the Specific Purpose Checklist on page 16 of this
    workbook? _____

6. What is your central idea? _____
    _____
    _____

7. Can you answer yes to all the questions on the Central Idea Checklist on page 17 of this
    workbook? _____

8. What method(s) of gaining attention do you use in the introduction? _____
    _____

9. How do you establish your credibility in the introduction? _____
    _____
    _____

- over -

10. Write the preview statement you will use in your introduction. _____

_____

_____

_____

11. Can you answer yes to all the questions on the Speech Introduction Checklist on page 39 of this workbook? _____

12. What method of organization do you use in the speech? _____

13. State in full sentences the main points to be developed in the body of your speech.

_____

_____

_____

_____

_____

14. Can you answer yes to all the questions on the Main Points Checklist on page 37 of this workbook? _____

15. What steps have you taken to adapt the content of your speech so it will be clear and interesting to your audience? Be specific.

_____

_____

_____

_____

_____

16. What method(s) of reinforcing your central idea do you use in the conclusion?

_____

_____

17. Can you answer yes to all the questions on the Speech Conclusion Checklist on page 40 of this workbook? _____

INFORMATIVE SPEECH TOPICS

As your textbook explains, there are limitless possibilities for speech topics—including topics you already know a lot about, topics you want to learn more about, and topics you discover through one or another brainstorming procedure. If you are having trouble coming up with a topic for your informative speech, check pages 76-81 of the textbook for advice. The topics listed below are meant to provide an additional spur to your creativity as you think about a subject for your speech. For more possible topics, check the Topic Finder in the online Speech Tools for Chapter 4 at connectlucas.com.

advertising	flamenco dancing	oriental rugs
aerobics	fly fishing	Palestine
African literature	Geronimo	parenting
Amelia Earhardt	ginsing	pets
animal behavior	glass	photography
antique furniture	graffiti	physical therapy
artificial intelligence	guitars	Picasso
asteroids	gymnastics	plastic surgery
asthma	Habitat for Humanity	pyramids
Aztecs	headaches	Quakers
bagpipes	homeopathy	quicksand
ballet	horse racing	robots
bats	hurricanes	rock climbing
Beijing	insomnia	rodeos
bicycles	interior design	ROTC
birth order	inventions	Russian culture
braiding	Iraq	sharks
Buddhism	Japanese tea ceremony	sleep deprivation
cartography	jazz	Spain
Chinese New Year	job interviews	spiders
chiropractic	Judaism	stock market
civil rights movement	kayaking	stress
Cleopatra	Koran	study abroad
cooking	Kwanzaa	sushi
Costa Rica	landscape architecture	table tennis
cryonics	laughter	tattoos
dams	lizards	television news
Dead Sea scrolls	Malcolm X	Thailand
diamonds	martial arts	tobacco
diets	military service	Trail of Tears
dream catchers	motorcycles	urban planning
druids	mushrooms	vegetarianism
earthquakes	mythology	Venice
electoral college	music therapy	volcanoes
Ellis Island	national parks	water
engineering	New Zealand	women's health
extraterrestrial intelligence	nursing	xerography
fencing	nutrition	Yosemite
fertility drugs	opera	youth sports
fire prevention	Olympic Games	zoos

INFORMATIVE SPEECH SELF-ASSESSMENT

Your task is to review your informative speech and to reach a full, objective assessment of its major strengths and weaknesses. Write a thoughtful evaluation of the speech in full-sentence and paragraph form with an introduction and a conclusion.

Be specific and concrete in your comments. Note in particular the areas in which you believe you did especially well and those areas in which you want to make special improvement in the next speech. Explain why you had difficulty with certain aspects of this speech and indicate the specific steps you will take to improve your next presentation.

Use the following questions to guide your self-assessment, though you do not need to answer each question individually in your paper. Be specific and concrete in your comments.

Topic and Purpose
Was the topic appropriate for the audience and the occasion?
Did you have a clear specific purpose that you could accomplish in the allotted time?

Organization
Was the speech well organized?
Did you fulfill all the major functions of a speech introduction?
Did you fulfill all the major objectives of a speech conclusion?
Were the main points of the body clear and easy to follow?
Did you use connectives effectively?

Supporting Materials, Audience Adaptation, and Language
Did you conduct adequate research when preparing the speech?
Did you adapt your speech so it would be relevant and interesting to your audience?
Did you follow the criteria in your textbook for the effective use of supporting materials?
Did you make a conscious effort to use clear, nontechnical language?

Delivery and Visual Aids
Did you begin and end your speech without rushing?
Did you use pauses, rate, pitch, and vocal variety effectively in delivering the speech?
Did your physical action add to or detract from the speech?
Did you maintain strong eye contact throughout the speech?
If you used visual aids, were they carefully prepared and smoothly integrated into the speech?
Did you follow the guidelines in your textbook for presenting visual aids?

Overall Assessment
What were you most pleased with in the speech? What were you least pleased with?
If you had an opportunity to deliver this speech again next week, what changes would you make? Be
    specific.

PERSUASIVE SPEECH TOPICS

As your textbook explains, there are limitless possibilities for speech topics—including topics you already know a lot about, topics you want to learn more about, and topics that you discover through one or another brainstorming procedure. If you are having trouble coming up with a topic for your persuasive speech, check pages 76-81 of the textbook for advice. The topics listed below are meant to provide an additional spur to your creativity as you think about a subject for your speech. For more possible topics, check the Topic Finder in the online Speech Tools for Chapter 4 at connectlucas.com.

adoption laws	education reform	nuclear weapons
advertising in schools	electoral college	nurse shortage
affirmative action	emergency rooms	organ donation
age discrimination	endangered species	personal health
agriculture	environmental pollution	prison system
AIDS	fire prevention	privacy laws
airbags	food safety	pesticides
airplane safety	foreign aid	political corruption
alcohol abuse	funding for the arts	poverty
alternate energy sources	gambling	pornography
animal testing	gay rights	prayer in schools
bilingual education	genetic engineering	prostitution
boat safety	global warming	public transportation
breast cancer	gun control	responsible journalism
campaign financing	health laboratories	road rage
campus safety	home schooling	school-bus safety
censorship	homelessness	school choice
chewing tobacco	human rights	sex education
child abuse	hunger	sickle-cell anemia
child labor	illiteracy	smokeless tobacco
child-custody laws	identity theft	Social Security
church-state separation	immigration laws	space exploration
cloning	international terrorism	speech codes
coastal erosion	Internet security	speed limits
college athletics	insanity defense	standardized tests
college tuition	juvenile murderers	student loans
community service	labor laws	sweatshops
consumer rights	logging	telephone deregulation
court system	mail-order fraud	television violence
crime prevention	managed care	tenants' rights
death penalty	mass transportation	truth in advertising
decaying bridges	medical malpractice	tuberculosis
diplomatic immunity	Middle East	United Nations
disability laws	mining	vandalism
discarded computers	minimum wage	victims' rights
DNA fingerprinting	music ratings	volunteering
doctor-assisted suicide	national defense	voting in elections
domestic violence	national health system	water purity
drug laws	national parks	water rights
drunk driving	noise pollution	women in the military

FACT, VALUE, POLICY WORKSHEET

Below are four specific purpose statements for persuasive speeches. In each case explain whether the speech associated with it concerns a question of fact, a question of value, or a question of policy. Then rewrite the specific purpose statement to make it appropriate for a speech about one of the other two kinds of questions. For instance, if the original purpose statement is about a question of policy, write a new specific purpose statement that deals with the same topic as either a question of fact or a question of value.

1.   To persuade my audience to get training in CPR.

    A.   Does this specific purpose deal with a question of fact, value, or policy? _____

    B.   Rewritten specific purpose statement: _____

        _____

        _____

2.   To persuade my audience that pornography is a major cause of violence against women.

    A.   Does this specific purpose deal with a question of fact, value, or policy? _____

    B.   Rewritten specific purpose statement: _____

        _____

        _____

3.   To persuade my audience that a national ban on private ownership of all kinds of guns should be adopted to help decrease violence.

    A.   Does this specific purpose deal with a question of fact, value, or policy? _____

    B.   Rewritten specific purpose statement: _____

        _____

        _____

4.   To persuade my audience that it is unethical for U.S. clothing companies to employ foreign workers at substandard wages.

    A.   Does this specific purpose deal with a question of fact, value, or policy? _____

    B.   Rewritten specific purpose statement: _____

        _____

        _____

PERSUASIVE SPEECH PREPARATION WORKSHEET

Name _____ Section _____

1. What is the topic of your speech? _____

2. Are you speaking on a question of fact, value, or policy? _____

3. What is your specific purpose statement? _____

    _____

    _____

4. Can you answer yes to all the questions on the Specific Purpose Checklist on page 16 of this
    workbook? _____

5. Is your speech meant to achieve passive agreement or immediate action from your audience?

    _____

6. What is your central idea? _____

    _____

    _____

7. Can you answer yes to all the questions on the Central Idea Checklist on page 17 of this
    workbook? _____

8. What is the target audience for your speech? How will you adapt your speech to be persuasive to
    your target audience? Be specific.

    _____

    _____

    _____

    _____

9. What method(s) of gaining attention do you use in the introduction? _____

    _____

    _____

10. How do you establish your credibility in the introduction? _____

    _____

    _____

    _____

11. Write the preview statement you will use in your introduction. _____

    _____

    _____

    _____

12. Can you answer yes to all the questions on the Speech Introduction Checklist on page 39 of this workbook? _____

13. What method of organization do you use in the speech? _____

14. State in full sentences the main points to be developed in the body of your speech.

    _____

    _____

    _____

    _____

    _____

15. Can you answer yes to all the questions on the Main Points Checklist on page 37 of this workbook? _____

16. What supporting materials do you use in developing each main point? Be specific.

    _____

    _____

    _____

    _____

    _____

17. Can you answer yes to all the questions on the Evidence Checklist on page 59 of this workbook? _____

18. What steps have you taken to answer potential objections that your audience may have to your position? Be specific.

    _____

    _____

    _____

    _____

19. What method(s) of reinforcing your central idea do you use in the conclusion?

    _____

    _____

EVIDENCE CHECKLIST

		Yes	No
1.	Are all of my major claims supported by evidence?	❑	❑
2.	Do I use sufficient evidence to convince my audience of my claims?	❑	❑
3.	Is my evidence stated in specific rather than general terms?	❑	❑
4.	Do I use evidence that is new to my audience?	❑	❑
5.	Is my evidence from credible, unbiased sources?	❑	❑
6.	Do I identify the sources of my evidence?	❑	❑
7.	Is my evidence clearly linked to each point that it is meant to prove?	❑	❑
8.	Do I provide evidence to answer possible objections the audience may have to my position?	❑	❑

FALLACIES WORKSHEET

Identify the fallacy in each of the following statements and, in each case, explain why the statement is fallacious.

1.   I don't see any reason to wear a helmet when I ride a bike. Everyone bikes without a helmet.

2.   It's ridiculous to worry about protecting America's national parks against pollution and overuse when innocent people are being killed by terrorists.

3.   There can be no doubt that the Great Depression was caused by Herbert Hoover. He became President in March 1929, and the stock market crashed just seven months later.

4.   If we allow the school board to spend money remodeling the gymnasium, next they will want to build a new school and give all the teachers a huge raise. Taxes will soar so high that businesses will leave and then there will be no jobs for anyone in this town.

5.   Raising a child is just like having a pet—you need to feed it, play with it, and everything will be fine.

6.   I can't support Representative Frey's proposal for campaign finance reform. After all, he was kicked out of law school for cheating on an exam.

7.   One nonsmoker, interviewed at a restaurant, said, "I can eat dinner just fine even though people around me are smoking." Another, responding to a *Los Angeles Times* survey, said, "I don't see what all the fuss is about. My wife has smoked for years and it has never bothered me." We can see, then, that secondhand smoke does not cause a problem for most nonsmokers.

8.   Our school must either increase tuition or cut back on library services for students.

SPEECH OUTLINE IN MONROE'S MOTIVATED SEQUENCE

A Friend in Need

Specific Purpose: To persuade my audience to volunteer time to help needy elderly people remain in their homes.

Central Idea: By participating in a volunteer program, college students can help needy elderly people continue to live independently in their homes.

Introduction

[Attention]
I.   Story of Loretta Olson, an 85-year-old woman who suffers from Alzheimer's disease.

II.   During my freshman year, I volunteered six hours a week to help Loretta remain independent in her home.

III.   Like Loretta, there are millions of elderly Americans who need help to remain independent in their homes.

IV.   In my class survey, all but two of you said you have living grandparents, and seven of you said you have grandparents who live alone.

V.   Today I would like to persuade you to help solve the problems facing less fortunate elderly Americans by volunteering time to help them remain independent in their homes.

(Transition: Let's begin by addressing the problems that can occur among this group of people.)

Body

[Need]
I.   There are two problems that can occur when elderly people living alone do not get the companionship and care they need.

A.   The first problem is that elderly people may not be able to meet all of their physical needs.

1.   Example of an 87-year-old woman whom I helped as a volunteer.

2.   Like this woman, many elderly people can live alone but need help with cleaning, food preparation, and transportation.

B.   The second problem is suicide.

1.   According to the National Center for Vital Statistics, people age 75 and older have the highest rate of suicide compared to all other groups.

2.   That high suicide rate stems from three major causes: helplessness, hopelessness, and haplessness.

a.   Helplessness describes the feelings of powerlessness some elderly people feel upon realizing they're losing their physical and mental vigor.

b.   Hopelessness is associated with depression caused by the realization of the onset of old age.

c.   Haplessness refers to a series of repeated losses, such as loss of earnings, friends, and family.

(Transition: Now that we have talked about the two major problems facing elderly people who do not get the companionship and care they need, let's talk about what we can do to help solve these problems.)

[Satisfaction]   II.   As individuals, we can help solve these problems by getting involved with a volunteer program that assists elderly people who need help living at home.
    A.   Here in Wisconsin, the Community Options Program is designed to help the elderly and people with disabilities stay out of nursing homes.
    B.   Right here in Madison, the Independent Living program provides companionship and assistance for elderly people who live at home.

[Visualization]   III.   It is practical and rewarding for college students to get involved with such programs.
    A.   You decide how much time to volunteer based on your individual schedule.
        1.   You can volunteer for as few as one or two hours a week.
        2.   You can volunteer for as many as forty hours a week.
    B.   You will experience great personal gratification by helping people less fortunate than yourself.
    C.   You can even receive financial assistance for participating in some volunteer programs.
        1.   Both the state-run Community Option Program and the federally-funded Title 19 Program offer financial assistance to people who participate.
        2.   This assistance can run from reimbursement for your travel expenses to an actual salary for certain kinds of work.

Conclusion

[Action]   I.   I am urging you to volunteer time to help needy elderly people remain independent in their homes.
    II.   Spending time with elderly people living alone can help them meet their physical and emotional needs.
    III.   You can adjust the time you spend to fit your schedule, you can get great personal gratification from volunteering, and you can receive monetary benefits as well.
    IV.   But most important, Loretta Olson—and millions like her—will be forever thankful for your efforts.

PERSUASIVE SPEECH SELF-ASSESSMENT

Your task is to review your persuasive speech and to reach a full, objective assessment of its major strengths and weaknesses. Write a thoughtful evaluation of the speech in full-sentence and paragraph form with an introduction and a conclusion.

Be specific and concrete in your comments. Note in particular the areas in which you believe you did especially well and those areas in which you want to make special improvement in the next speech. Explain why you had difficulty with certain aspects of this speech and indicate the specific steps you will take to improve your next presentation.

Use the following questions to guide your self-assessment, though you do not need to answer each question individually in your paper. Be specific and concrete in your comments.

Topic and Purpose
    Was the topic appropriate for the audience and occasion?
    Did you have a clear specific purpose that you could accomplish in the allotted time?

Organization
    Was the speech well organized?
    Did you fulfill all the major functions of a speech introduction?
    Did you fulfill all the major objectives of a speech conclusion?
    Were the main points of the body clear and easy to follow?
    Did you use connectives effectively?

Supporting Materials, Audience Adaptation, and Language
    Did you conduct adequate research when preparing the speech?
    Were your ideas well supported and explained?
    If you spoke on a question of policy, did you demonstrate a need to change current policy?
    Did you present a clear plan to solve the need? Did you prove the practicality of your plan?
    Did you follow the criteria in your textbook for the effective use of supporting materials?
    Did you identify the target audience for your speech?
    Did you use evidence to answer the potential objections of your target audience?
    Did you present your ideas in clear, vivid, accurate, and appropriate language?

Delivery and Visual Aids
    Did you begin and end your speech without rushing?
    Did you use pauses, rate, pitch, and vocal variety effectively in delivering the speech?
    Did your physical action add to or detract from the speech?
    Did you maintain strong eye contact throughout the speech?
    If you used visual aids, were they carefully prepared and smoothly integrated into the speech?
    Did you follow the guidelines in your textbook for presenting visual aids?

Overall Assessment
    What were you most pleased with in the speech? What were you least pleased with?
    If you had an opportunity to deliver this speech again next week, what changes would you make?
        Be specific.

SPEECH OF INTRODUCTION OBSERVATION WORKSHEET

Your name _____

Name of speaker you observed _____

Where was the speech presented? _____

Who was the speaker introducing? _____

Evaluate the speech of introduction as follows:

1.   How long was the speech? Was it too long? Too short? About right? Explain.

2.   As far as you can tell, was the speech accurate in its remarks about the main speaker? Explain.

3.   Was the speech well adapted to the occasion? Explain.

4.   Was the speech well adapted to the main speaker? Explain.

5.   Was the speech well adapted to the audience? Explain.

6.   Did the speech create a sense of anticipation and drama about the main speaker? Explain.

SPECIAL-OCCASION SPEECH SELF-ASSESSMENT

Your task is to review your special-occasion speech and to reach a full, objective assessment of its major strengths and weaknesses. Write a thoughtful, objective evaluation of the speech in full-sentence and paragraph form with an introduction and a conclusion.

Be specific and concrete in your comments. Note in particular the areas in which you believe you did especially well and those areas in which you want to make special improvement in the next speech. Explain why you had difficulty with certain aspects of this speech, and indicate the specific steps you plan to take to improve your next presentation.

Use the following questions to guide your self-assessment, though you do not need to answer each question individually in your paper. Be specific and concrete in your comments.

Topic
    Was the topic appropriate for the occasion?
    Was the topic appropriate for the audience?
    Did you deal with the topic creatively?

Organization
    Did your introduction gain the attention and interest of the audience?
    Were the main ideas of the speech easy to follow?
    Did you use connectives effectively?
    Did you conclude the speech in a memorable fashion?

Language
    Was your language clear and concrete?
    Was your language vivid and colorful?
    Was your language appropriate to the topic, audience, and occasion?

Delivery
    Did you begin and end your speech without rushing?
    Did you use pauses, rate, pitch, and vocal variety effectively in delivering the speech?
    Did your physical action add to or detract from the speech?
    Did you maintain strong eye contact throughout the speech?

Overall Assessment
    What were you most pleased with in the speech? What were you least pleased with?
    If you had an opportunity to deliver this speech again next week, what changes would you
        make? Be specific.

REFLECTIVE THINKING METHOD CHECKLIST

	Yes	No
1. Did the group clearly define the problem for discussion?	❏	❏
2. Did the group phrase the question for discussion as a question of policy?	❏	❏
3. Did the group phrase the question for discussion as clearly as possible?	❏	❏
4. Did the group phrase the question for discussion so as to allow for a wide variety of answers?	❏	❏
5. Did the group phrase the question for discussion in an unbiased manner?	❏	❏
6. Did the group phrase the question for discussion as a single question?	❏	❏
7. Did the group analyze the problem thoroughly before attempting to map out solutions?	❏	❏
8. Did the group establish criteria for an ideal solution to the problem before discussing specific solutions?	❏	❏
9. Did the group brainstorm to generate a wide range of potential solutions to the problem?	❏	❏
10. Did the group evaluate each potential solution in light of the criteria for an ideal solution?	❏	❏
11. Did the group make a determined effort to reach consensus with regard to the best solution?	❏	❏
12. Did the group achieve consensus?	❏	❏

GROUP DISCUSSION SELF-ASSESSMENT

Your task is to reach a full, objective assessment of the major strengths and weaknesses of your small group and of your performance in the group. Write a thoughtful, objective evaluation in full-sentence and paragraph form with an introduction and a conclusion.

Use the following questions to guide your self-assessment, though you do not need to answer each question individually in your paper. Be specific and concrete in your comments.

Leadership

Did your group have a designated leader?

If you did not have a designated leader, what kind of leadership developed in the group?

Which members were most effective in meeting the group's procedural needs?

Which members were most effective in meeting the group's task needs?

Which members were most effective in meeting the group's maintenance needs?

Responsibilities of Group Members

How fully did members commit themselves to the goals of the group?

How well did members carry out their individual assignments?

Did the group avoid interpersonal conflict by keeping disagreement at the task level?

Did vocal members encourage full participation by other members of the group?

Did group members work to keep discussion on track?

Use of the Reflective-Thinking Method

Did the group define the question for discussion clearly?

Did the group analyze the problem thoroughly before attempting to map out solutions?

Did the group establish criteria for an ideal solution?

Did the group brainstorm to generate a wide range of potential solutions?

Did the group evaluate each potential solution in light of the criteria for an ideal solution?

Did the group make a determined effort to reach consensus about the best solution?

Did the group achieve consensus? Why or why not?

Overall Evaluation

Are you satisfied with the work of the group and with your role in the group?

If the group were to start its project over again, what changes would you recommend to help the group work more effectively? Be specific.

SPEECH EVALUATION

FORMS

SPEECH EVALUATION FORM

Speaker _____

Topic _____

Rate the speaker on each point: *E-excellent*   *G-good*   *A-average*   *F-fair*   *P-poor*

INTRODUCTION

Gained attention and interest	E G A F P
Introduced topic clearly	E G A F P
Related topic to audience	E G A F P
Established credibility	E G A F P
Previewed body of speech	E G A F P

BODY

Main points clear	E G A F P
Main points fully supported	E G A F P
Organization well planned	E G A F P
Language accurate	E G A F P
Language clear	E G A F P
Language appropriate	E G A F P
Connectives effective	E G A F P

CONCLUSION

Prepared audience for ending	E G A F P
Reinforced central idea	E G A F P
Vivid ending	E G A F P

DELIVERY

Began speech without rushing	E G A F P
Maintained strong eye contact	E G A F P
Avoided distracting mannerisms	E G A F P
Articulated words clearly	E G A F P
Used pauses effectively	E G A F P
Used vocal variety to add impact	E G A F P
Prepared visual aids well	E G A F P
Presented visual aids well	E G A F P
Communicated enthusiasm for topic	E G A F P
Departed from lectern without rushing	E G A F P

OVERALL EVALUATION

Met assignment	E G A F P
Topic challenging	E G A F P
Specific purpose well chosen	E G A F P
Message adapted to audience	E G A F P
Speech completed within time limit	E G A F P
Held interest of audience	E G A F P

What did the speaker do most effectively? _____

_____

_____

What should the speaker pay special attention to next time? _____

_____

_____

General Comments: _____

_____

_____

_____

SPEECH EVALUATION FORM

Speaker _____

Topic _____

Rate the speaker on each point: *E-excellent*   *G-good*   *A-average*   *F-fair*   *P-poor*

INTRODUCTION

Gained attention and interest	E G A F P
Introduced topic clearly	E G A F P
Related topic to audience	E G A F P
Established credibility	E G A F P
Previewed body of speech	E G A F P

BODY

Main points clear	E G A F P
Main points fully supported	E G A F P
Organization well planned	E G A F P
Language accurate	E G A F P
Language clear	E G A F P
Language appropriate	E G A F P
Connectives effective	E G A F P

CONCLUSION

Prepared audience for ending	E G A F P
Reinforced central idea	E G A F P
Vivid ending	E G A F P

DELIVERY

Began speech without rushing	E G A F P
Maintained strong eye contact	E G A F P
Avoided distracting mannerisms	E G A F P
Articulated words clearly	E G A F P
Used pauses effectively	E G A F P
Used vocal variety to add impact	E G A F P
Prepared visual aids well	E G A F P
Presented visual aids well	E G A F P
Communicated enthusiasm for topic	E G A F P
Departed from lectern without rushing	E G A F P

OVERALL EVALUATION

Met assignment	E G A F P
Topic challenging	E G A F P
Specific purpose well chosen	E G A F P
Message adapted to audience	E G A F P
Speech completed within time limit	E G A F P
Held interest of audience	E G A F P

_____

What did the speaker do most effectively? _____

_____

_____

What should the speaker pay special attention to next time? _____

_____

_____

General Comments: _____

_____

_____

_____

SPEECH EVALUATION FORM

Speaker _____

Topic _____

Rate the speaker on each point: *E-excellent*   *G-good*   *A-average*   *F-fair*   *P-poor*

INTRODUCTION		**DELIVERY**	
Gained attention and interest	E G A F P	Began speech without rushing	E G A F P
Introduced topic clearly	E G A F P	Maintained strong eye contact	E G A F P
Related topic to audience	E G A F P	Avoided distracting mannerisms	E G A F P
Established credibility	E G A F P	Articulated words clearly	E G A F P
Previewed body of speech	E G A F P	Used pauses effectively	E G A F P
		Used vocal variety to add impact	E G A F P
BODY		Prepared visual aids well	E G A F P
Main points clear	E G A F P	Presented visual aids well	E G A F P
Main points fully supported	E G A F P	Communicated enthusiasm for topic	E G A F P
Organization well planned	E G A F P	Departed from lectern without rushing	E G A F P
Language accurate	E G A F P		
Language clear	E G A F P	**OVERALL EVALUATION**	
Language appropriate	E G A F P	Met assignment	E G A F P
Connectives effective	E G A F P	Topic challenging	E G A F P
		Specific purpose well chosen	E G A F P
CONCLUSION		Message adapted to audience	E G A F P
Prepared audience for ending	E G A F P	Speech completed within time limit	E G A F P
Reinforced central idea	E G A F P	Held interest of audience	E G A F P
Vivid ending	E G A F P		

What did the speaker do most effectively? _____

_____

_____

What should the speaker pay special attention to next time? _____

_____

_____

General Comments: _____

_____

_____

_____

SPEECH EVALUATION FORM

Speaker _____

Topic _____

Rate the speaker on each point.   E—excellent   G—good   A—average   F—fair   P—poor

INTRODUCTION

Gained attention and interest	E G A F P
Introduced topic clearly	E G A F P
Related topic to audience	E G A F P
Established credibility	E G A F P
Previewed body of speech	E G A F P

BODY

Main points clear	E G A F P
Main points fully supported	E G A F P
Organization well planned	E G A F P
Language accurate	E G A F P
Language clear	E G A F P
Language appropriate	E G A F P
Connectives effective	E G A F P

CONCLUSION

Prepared audience for ending	E G A F P
Reinforced central idea	E G A F P
Vivid ending	E G A F P

DELIVERY

Began speech without rushing	E G A F P
Maintained strong eye contact	E G A F P
Avoided distracting mannerisms	E G A F P
Articulated words clearly	E G A F P
Used pauses effectively	E G A F P
Used vocal variety to add impact	E G A F P
Prepared visual aids well	E G A F P
Presented visual aids well	E G A F P
Communicated enthusiasm for topic	E G A F P
Departed from lectern without rushing	E G A F P

OVERALL EVALUATION

Met assignment	E G A F P
Topic challenging	E G A F P
Specific purpose well chosen	E G A F P
Message adapted to audience	E G A F P
Speech completed within time limit	E G A F P
Held interest of audience	E G A F P

What did the speaker do most effectively? _____

What should the speaker pay special attention to next time? _____

Overall comments: _____

SPEECH EVALUATION FORM

Speaker _____

Topic _____

Rate the speaker on each point: *E-excellent*   *G-good*   *A-average*   *F-fair*   *P-poor*

INTRODUCTION

Gained attention and interest	E G A F P
Introduced topic clearly	E G A F P
Related topic to audience	E G A F P
Established credibility	E G A F P
Previewed body of speech	E G A F P

BODY

Main points clear	E G A F P
Main points fully supported	E G A F P
Organization well planned	E G A F P
Language accurate	E G A F P
Language clear	E G A F P
Language appropriate	E G A F P
Connectives effective	E G A F P

CONCLUSION

Prepared audience for ending	E G A F P
Reinforced central idea	E G A F P
Vivid ending	E G A F P

DELIVERY

Began speech without rushing	E G A F P
Maintained strong eye contact	E G A F P
Avoided distracting mannerisms	E G A F P
Articulated words clearly	E G A F P
Used pauses effectively	E G A F P
Used vocal variety to add impact	E G A F P
Prepared visual aids well	E G A F P
Presented visual aids well	E G A F P
Communicated enthusiasm for topic	E G A F P
Departed from lectern without rushing	E G A F P

OVERALL EVALUATION

Met assignment	E G A F P
Topic challenging	E G A F P
Specific purpose well chosen	E G A F P
Message adapted to audience	E G A F P
Speech completed within time limit	E G A F P
Held interest of audience	E G A F P

_____

What did the speaker do most effectively? _____

_____

_____

What should the speaker pay special attention to next time? _____

_____

_____

General Comments: _____

_____

_____

_____

SPEECH EVALUATION FORM

Speaker: _____

Topic: _____

Rate the speaker on each point: Excellent Good Average Fair Poor

INTRODUCTION

Gained attention and interest   E G A F P
Introduced topic clearly   E G A F P
Related topic to audience   E G A F P
Established credibility   E G A F P
Previewed body of speech   E G A F P

BODY

Main points clear   E G A F P
Main points fully supported   E G A F P
Organization well planned   E G A F P
Language accurate   E G A F P
Language clear   E G A F P
Strong transitions   E G A F P
Connectives effective   E G A F P

CONCLUSION

Prepared audience for ending   E G A F P
Reinforced central idea   E G A F P
Vivid ending   E G A F P

DELIVERY

Began speech without rushing   E G A F P
Maintained strong eye contact   E G A F P
Avoided distracting mannerisms   E G A F P
Articulated words clearly   E G A F P
Used pauses effectively   E G A F P
Used vocal variety to add impact   E G A F P
Presented visual aids well   E G A F P
Communicated enthusiasm for topic   E G A F P
Departed from lectern without rushing   E G A F P

OVERALL EVALUATION

Met assignment   E G A F P
Topic challenging   E G A F P
Specific purpose well chosen   E G A F P
Message adapted to audience   E G A F P
Speech completed within time limit   E G A F P
Held my interest and attention   E G A F P

What did the speaker do most effectively?

_____

_____

What should the speaker give special attention to next time?

_____

_____

General comments:

_____

_____

SPEECH EVALUATION FORM

Speaker _____

Topic _____

Rate the speaker on each point: *E-excellent*   *G-good*   *A-average*   *F-fair*   *P-poor*

INTRODUCTION

Gained attention and interest	E G A F P
Introduced topic clearly	E G A F P
Related topic to audience	E G A F P
Established credibility	E G A F P
Previewed body of speech	E G A F P

BODY

Main points clear	E G A F P
Main points fully supported	E G A F P
Organization well planned	E G A F P
Language accurate	E G A F P
Language clear	E G A F P
Language appropriate	E G A F P
Connectives effective	E G A F P

CONCLUSION

Prepared audience for ending	E G A F P
Reinforced central idea	E G A F P
Vivid ending	E G A F P

DELIVERY

Began speech without rushing	E G A F P
Maintained strong eye contact	E G A F P
Avoided distracting mannerisms	E G A F P
Articulated words clearly	E G A F P
Used pauses effectively	E G A F P
Used vocal variety to add impact	E G A F P
Prepared visual aids well	E G A F P
Presented visual aids well	E G A F P
Communicated enthusiasm for topic	E G A F P
Departed from lectern without rushing	E G A F P

OVERALL EVALUATION

Met assignment	E G A F P
Topic challenging	E G A F P
Specific purpose well chosen	E G A F P
Message adapted to audience	E G A F P
Speech completed within time limit	E G A F P
Held interest of audience	E G A F P

_____

What did the speaker do most effectively? _____

_____

_____

What should the speaker pay special attention to next time? _____

_____

_____

General Comments: _____

_____

_____

_____

SPEECH EVALUATION FORM

Speaker _____

Topic _____

Rate the speaker on each point.   E=excellent   G=good   A=average   F=fair   P=poor

INTRODUCTION

Gained attention and interest	E G A F P
Introduced topic clearly	E G A F P
Related topic to audience	E G A F P
Defined and credibility	E G A F P
Previewed body of speech	E G A F P

BODY

Main point clear	E G A F P
Main points fully supported	E G A F P
Organization well planned	E G A F P
Language accurate	E G A F P
Language clear	E G A F P
Language appropriate	E G A F P
Connectives effective	E G A F P

CONCLUSION

Prepared audience for ending	E G A F P
Reinforced central idea	E G A F P
Vivid ending	E G A F P

DELIVERY

Began speech without rushing	E G A F P
Maintained among eye contact	E G A F P
Avoided distracting mannerisms	E G A F P
Articulated words clearly	E G A F P
Used pauses effectively	E G A F P
Used vocal variety to add impact	E G A F P
Prepared visual aids well	E G A F P
Presented visual aid well	E G A F P
Communicated enthusiasm for topic	E G A F P
Departed from lectern without rushing	E G A F P

OVERALL EVALUATION

Met assignment	E G A F P
Topic challenging	E G A F P
Specific purpose well chosen	E G A F P
Message adapted to audience	E G A F P
Speech completed within time limit	E G A F P
Held interest of audience	E G A F P

What did the speaker do most effectively?

What should the speaker pay special attention to next time?

General Comments:

SPEECH EVALUATION FORM

Speaker _____

Topic _____

Rate the speaker on each point: *E-excellent*   *G-good*   *A-average*   *F-fair*   *P-poor*

INTRODUCTION

Gained attention and interest	E G A F P
Introduced topic clearly	E G A F P
Related topic to audience	E G A F P
Established credibility	E G A F P
Previewed body of speech	E G A F P

BODY

Main points clear	E G A F P
Main points fully supported	E G A F P
Organization well planned	E G A F P
Language accurate	E G A F P
Language clear	E G A F P
Language appropriate	E G A F P
Connectives effective	E G A F P

CONCLUSION

Prepared audience for ending	E G A F P
Reinforced central idea	E G A F P
Vivid ending	E G A F P

DELIVERY

Began speech without rushing	E G A F P
Maintained strong eye contact	E G A F P
Avoided distracting mannerisms	E G A F P
Articulated words clearly	E G A F P
Used pauses effectively	E G A F P
Used vocal variety to add impact	E G A F P
Prepared visual aids well	E G A F P
Presented visual aids well	E G A F P
Communicated enthusiasm for topic	E G A F P
Departed from lectern without rushing	E G A F P

OVERALL EVALUATION

Met assignment	E G A F P
Topic challenging	E G A F P
Specific purpose well chosen	E G A F P
Message adapted to audience	E G A F P
Speech completed within time limit	E G A F P
Held interest of audience	E G A F P

What did the speaker do most effectively? _____

_____

What should the speaker pay special attention to next time? _____

_____

General Comments: _____

_____

_____

_____

SPEECH EVALUATION FORM

Speaker _____

Topic _____

Rate the speaker on each point: E—Excellent G—Good A—Average F—Fair P—Poor

INTRODUCTION

	E	G	A	F	P
Gained attention and interest					
Introduced topic clearly					
Related topic to audience					
Established credibility					
Previewed body of speech					

BODY

	E	G	A	F	P
Main points clear					
Main points fully supported					
Organization well planned					
Language accurate					
Language clear					
Language appropriate					
Connectives effective					

CONCLUSION

	E	G	A	F	P
Prepared audience for ending					
Reinforced central idea					
Vivid ending					

DELIVERY

	E	G	A	F	P
Began speech without rushing					
Maintained strong eye contact					
Avoided distracting mannerisms					
Articulated words clearly					
Used pauses effectively					
Used vocal variety to add impact					
Prepared visual aids well					
Presented visual aids well					
Communicated enthusiasm for topic					
Departed from lectern without rushing					

OVERALL EVALUATION

	E	G	A	F	P
Met assignment					
Topic challenging					
Specific purpose well chosen					
Message adapted to audience					
Speech completed within time limit					
Held interest of audience					

What did the speaker do most effectively?

_____

What should the speaker try to improve on next time?

_____

General comments:

_____

SPEECH EVALUATION FORM

Speaker _____

Topic _____

Rate the speaker on each point: *E-excellent   G-good   A-average   F-fair   P-poor*

INTRODUCTION

Gained attention and interest	E G A F P
Introduced topic clearly	E G A F P
Related topic to audience	E G A F P
Established credibility	E G A F P
Previewed body of speech	E G A F P

BODY

Main points clear	E G A F P
Main points fully supported	E G A F P
Organization well planned	E G A F P
Language accurate	E G A F P
Language clear	E G A F P
Language appropriate	E G A F P
Connectives effective	E G A F P

CONCLUSION

Prepared audience for ending	E G A F P
Reinforced central idea	E G A F P
Vivid ending	E G A F P

DELIVERY

Began speech without rushing	E G A F P
Maintained strong eye contact	E G A F P
Avoided distracting mannerisms	E G A F P
Articulated words clearly	E G A F P
Used pauses effectively	E G A F P
Used vocal variety to add impact	E G A F P
Prepared visual aids well	E G A F P
Presented visual aids well	E G A F P
Communicated enthusiasm for topic	E G A F P
Departed from lectern without rushing	E G A F P

OVERALL EVALUATION

Met assignment	E G A F P
Topic challenging	E G A F P
Specific purpose well chosen	E G A F P
Message adapted to audience	E G A F P
Speech completed within time limit	E G A F P
Held interest of audience	E G A F P

_____

What did the speaker do most effectively? _____

_____

_____

What should the speaker pay special attention to next time? _____

_____

_____

General Comments: _____

_____

_____

_____

SPEECH EVALUATION FORM

Speaker _____

Topic _____

Rate the speaker on each point: *E-excellent*   *G-good*   *A-average*   *F-fair*   *P-poor*

INTRODUCTION		**DELIVERY**	
Gained attention and interest	E G A F P	Began speech without rushing	E G A F P
Introduced topic clearly	E G A F P	Maintained strong eye contact	E G A F P
Related topic to audience	E G A F P	Avoided distracting mannerisms	E G A F P
Established credibility	E G A F P	Articulated words clearly	E G A F P
Previewed body of speech	E G A F P	Used pauses effectively	E G A F P
		Used vocal variety to add impact	E G A F P
BODY		Prepared visual aids well	E G A F P
Main points clear	E G A F P	Presented visual aids well	E G A F P
Main points fully supported	E G A F P	Communicated enthusiasm for topic	E G A F P
Organization well planned	E G A F P	Departed from lectern without rushing	E G A F P
Language accurate	E G A F P		
Language clear	E G A F P	**OVERALL EVALUATION**	
Language appropriate	E G A F P	Met assignment	E G A F P
Connectives effective	E G A F P	Topic challenging	E G A F P
		Specific purpose well chosen	E G A F P
CONCLUSION		Message adapted to audience	E G A F P
Prepared audience for ending	E G A F P	Speech completed within time limit	E G A F P
Reinforced central idea	E G A F P	Held interest of audience	E G A F P
Vivid ending	E G A F P		

What did the speaker do most effectively? _____

_____

What should the speaker pay special attention to next time? _____

_____

_____

General Comments: _____

_____

_____

_____

SPEECH EVALUATION FORM

Speaker _____

Topic _____

Rate the speaker on each point: E—Excellent   G—Good   A—Average   F—Fair   P—Poor

INTRODUCTION

Gained attention and interest	E	G	A	F	P
Introduced topic clearly	E	G	A	F	P
Related to the audience	E	G	A	F	P
Established credibility	E	G	A	F	P
Previewed the speech	E	G	A	F	P

BODY

Main points clear	E	G	A	F	P
Main points fully supported	E	G	A	F	P
Organization well structured	E	G	A	F	P
Language accurate	E	G	A	F	P
Language clear	E	G	A	F	P
Connectives effective	E	G	A	F	P

CONCLUSION

Prepared audience for ending	E	G	A	F	P
Reinforced central idea	E	G	A	F	P
Vivid ending	E	G	A	F	P

DELIVERY

Began speech without rushing	E	G	A	F	P
Maintained eye contact	E	G	A	F	P
Avoided distracting mannerisms	E	G	A	F	P
Articulated words clearly	E	G	A	F	P
Used pauses effectively	E	G	A	F	P
Used vocal variety to add impact	E	G	A	F	P
Presented visual aids well	E	G	A	F	P
Displayed enthusiasm for topic	E	G	A	F	P
Departed from lectern without rushing	E	G	A	F	P

OVERALL EVALUATION

Met assignment	E	G	A	F	P
Topic challenging	E	G	A	F	P
Specific purpose well chosen	E	G	A	F	P
Message adapted to audience	E	G	A	F	P
Speech completed within time limit	E	G	A	F	P
Held interest of audience	E	G	A	F	P

What did the speaker do well in this speech?

_____

_____

_____

What should the speaker pay special attention to next time?

_____

_____

_____

General Comments:

_____

_____

SPEECH EVALUATION FORM

Speaker _____

Topic _____

Rate the speaker on each point: *E-excellent*   *G-good*   *A-average*   *F-fair*   *P-poor*

INTRODUCTION

Gained attention and interest	E G A F P
Introduced topic clearly	E G A F P
Related topic to audience	E G A F P
Established credibility	E G A F P
Previewed body of speech	E G A F P

BODY

Main points clear	E G A F P
Main points fully supported	E G A F P
Organization well planned	E G A F P
Language accurate	E G A F P
Language clear	E G A F P
Language appropriate	E G A F P
Connectives effective	E G A F P

CONCLUSION

Prepared audience for ending	E G A F P
Reinforced central idea	E G A F P
Vivid ending	E G A F P

DELIVERY

Began speech without rushing	E G A F P
Maintained strong eye contact	E G A F P
Avoided distracting mannerisms	E G A F P
Articulated words clearly	E G A F P
Used pauses effectively	E G A F P
Used vocal variety to add impact	E G A F P
Prepared visual aids well	E G A F P
Presented visual aids well	E G A F P
Communicated enthusiasm for topic	E G A F P
Departed from lectern without rushing	E G A F P

OVERALL EVALUATION

Met assignment	E G A F P
Topic challenging	E G A F P
Specific purpose well chosen	E G A F P
Message adapted to audience	E G A F P
Speech completed within time limit	E G A F P
Held interest of audience	E G A F P

_____

What did the speaker do most effectively? _____

_____

_____

What should the speaker pay special attention to next time? _____

_____

_____

General Comments: _____

_____

_____

_____

SPEECH EVALUATION FORM

Speaker: _____

Topic: _____

Key: U unacceptable P poor A average G good E excellent

INTRODUCTION

Gained attention and interest	E	G	A	P	U
Introduced topic clearly	E	G	A	P	U
Related topic to audience	E	G	A	P	U
Established credibility	E	G	A	P	U
Previewed body of speech	E	G	A	P	U

BODY

Main points clear	E	G	A	P	U
Main points fully supported	E	G	A	P	U
Organization well planned	E	G	A	P	U
Language accurate	E	G	A	P	U
Language clear	E	G	A	P	U
Language appropriate	E	G	A	P	U
Connectives effective	E	G	A	P	U

CONCLUSION

Prepared audience for ending	E	G	A	P	U
Reinforced central idea	E	G	A	P	U
Vivid ending	E	G	A	P	U

DELIVERY

Began speech without rushing	E	G	A	P	U
Maintained strong eye contact	E	G	A	P	U
Avoided distracting mannerisms	E	G	A	P	U
Articulated words clearly	E	G	A	P	U
Used pauses effectively	E	G	A	P	U
Used vocal variety to add impact	E	G	A	P	U
Presented visual aids well	E	G	A	P	U
Presented visual aids well	E	G	A	P	U
Communicated enthusiasm for topic	E	G	A	P	U
Departed from lectern without rushing	E	G	A	P	U

OVERALL EVALUATION

Met assignment	E	G	A	P	U
Topic challenging	E	G	A	P	U
Specific purpose well chosen	E	G	A	P	U
Message adapted to audience	E	G	A	P	U
Speech completed in time limit	E	G	A	P	U
Held interest of audience	E	G	A	P	U

What did the speaker do most effectively? _____

What should the speaker pay special attention to next time? _____

General Comments: _____

SPEECH EVALUATION FORM

Speaker _____

Topic _____

Rate the speaker on each point: *E-excellent*   *G-good*   *A-average*   *F-fair*   *P-poor*

INTRODUCTION

Gained attention and interest	E G A F P
Introduced topic clearly	E G A F P
Related topic to audience	E G A F P
Established credibility	E G A F P
Previewed body of speech	E G A F P

BODY

Main points clear	E G A F P
Main points fully supported	E G A F P
Organization well planned	E G A F P
Language accurate	E G A F P
Language clear	E G A F P
Language appropriate	E G A F P
Connectives effective	E G A F P

CONCLUSION

Prepared audience for ending	E G A F P
Reinforced central idea	E G A F P
Vivid ending	E G A F P

DELIVERY

Began speech without rushing	E G A F P
Maintained strong eye contact	E G A F P
Avoided distracting mannerisms	E G A F P
Articulated words clearly	E G A F P
Used pauses effectively	E G A F P
Used vocal variety to add impact	E G A F P
Prepared visual aids well	E G A F P
Presented visual aids well	E G A F P
Communicated enthusiasm for topic	E G A F P
Departed from lectern without rushing	E G A F P

OVERALL EVALUATION

Met assignment	E G A F P
Topic challenging	E G A F P
Specific purpose well chosen	E G A F P
Message adapted to audience	E G A F P
Speech completed within time limit	E G A F P
Held interest of audience	E G A F P

_____

What did the speaker do most effectively? _____

_____

What should the speaker pay special attention to next time? _____

_____

General Comments: _____

_____

_____

SPEECH EVALUATION FORM

Speaker: _____

Topic: _____

Rate the speaker on each point: E (excellent)   G (good)   A (average)   F (fair)   P (poor)

INTRODUCTION

Gained attention and interest	E	G	A	F	P
Introduced topic clearly	E	G	A	F	P
Related topic to audience	E	G	A	F	P
Established credibility	E	G	A	F	P
Previewed body of speech	E	G	A	F	P

BODY

Main points clear	E	G	A	F	P
Main points fully supported	E	G	A	F	P
Organization well planned	E	G	A	F	P
Language accurate	E	G	A	F	P
Language clear	E	G	A	F	P
Language appropriate	E	G	A	F	P
Connectives effective	E	G	A	F	P

CONCLUSION

Prepared audience for ending	E	G	A	F	P
Reinforced central idea	E	G	A	F	P
Vivid ending	E	G	A	F	P

DELIVERY

Began speech without rushing	E	G	A	F	P
Maintained strong eye contact	E	G	A	F	P
Avoided distracting mannerisms	E	G	A	F	P
Articulated words clearly	E	G	A	F	P
Used pauses effectively	E	G	A	F	P
Used vocal variety to add impact	E	G	A	F	P
Prepared visual aids well	E	G	A	F	P
Presented visual aids well	E	G	A	F	P
Communicated enthusiasm for topic	E	G	A	F	P
Departed from lectern without rushing	E	G	A	F	P

OVERALL EVALUATION

Met assignment	E	G	A	F	P
Topic challenging	E	G	A	F	P
Specific purpose well chosen	E	G	A	F	P
Message adapted to audience	E	G	A	F	P
Speech completed within time limit	E	G	A	F	P
Held interest of audience	E	G	A	F	P

What did the speaker do most effectively?

_____

_____

What should the speaker pay special attention to next time?

_____

_____

General comments:

_____

_____

SPEECH EVALUATION FORM

Speaker _____

Topic _____

Rate the speaker on each point: *E-excellent*   *G-good*   *A-average*   *F-fair*   *P-poor*

INTRODUCTION

Gained attention and interest	E G A F P
Introduced topic clearly	E G A F P
Related topic to audience	E G A F P
Established credibility	E G A F P
Previewed body of speech	E G A F P

BODY

Main points clear	E G A F P
Main points fully supported	E G A F P
Organization well planned	E G A F P
Language accurate	E G A F P
Language clear	E G A F P
Language appropriate	E G A F P
Connectives effective	E G A F P

CONCLUSION

Prepared audience for ending	E G A F P
Reinforced central idea	E G A F P
Vivid ending	E G A F P

DELIVERY

Began speech without rushing	E G A F P
Maintained strong eye contact	E G A F P
Avoided distracting mannerisms	E G A F P
Articulated words clearly	E G A F P
Used pauses effectively	E G A F P
Used vocal variety to add impact	E G A F P
Prepared visual aids well	E G A F P
Presented visual aids well	E G A F P
Communicated enthusiasm for topic	E G A F P
Departed from lectern without rushing	E G A F P

OVERALL EVALUATION

Met assignment	E G A F P
Topic challenging	E G A F P
Specific purpose well chosen	E G A F P
Message adapted to audience	E G A F P
Speech completed within time limit	E G A F P
Held interest of audience	E G A F P

_____

What did the speaker do most effectively? _____

_____

_____

What should the speaker pay special attention to next time? _____

_____

_____

General Comments: _____

_____

_____

_____

SPEECH EVALUATION FORM

Speaker _____

Topic _____

Rate the speaker on each point: E=excellent   G=good   A=average   F=fair   P=poor

INTRODUCTION

Gained attention and interest   E G A F P
Introduced topic clearly   E G A F P
Related topic to audience   E G A F P
Established credibility   E G A F P
Reviewed body of speech   E G A F P

BODY

Main points clear   E G A F P
Main points fully supported   E G A F P
Organization well planned   E G A F P
Language accurate   E G A F P
Language clear   E G A F P
Language appropriate   E G A F P
Connectives effective   E G A F P

CONCLUSION

Prepared audience for ending   E G A F P
Reinforced central idea   E G A F P
Vivid ending   E G A F P

DELIVERY

Began speech without rushing   E G A F P
Maintained strong eye contact   E G A F P
Avoided distracting mannerisms   E G A F P
Articulated words clearly   E G A F P
Used pauses effectively   E G A F P
Used vocal variety to add impact   E G A F P
Prepared visual aid well   E G A F P
Presented visual aid well   E G A F P
Communicated enthusiasm for topic   E G A F P
Departed from lectern without rushing   E G A F P

OVERALL EVALUATION

Met assignment   E G A F P
Topic challenging   E G A F P
Specific purpose well chosen   E G A F P
Message adapted to audience   E G A F P
Speech completed within time limit   E G A F P
Held interest of audience   E G A F P

What did the speaker do most effectively? _____

What should the speaker pay special attention to next time? _____

General Comments: _____

SPEECH EVALUATION FORM

Speaker _____

Topic _____

Rate the speaker on each point: *E-excellent*   *G-good*   *A-average*   *F-fair*   *P-poor*

INTRODUCTION

Gained attention and interest	E G A F P
Introduced topic clearly	E G A F P
Related topic to audience	E G A F P
Established credibility	E G A F P
Previewed body of speech	E G A F P

BODY

Main points clear	E G A F P
Main points fully supported	E G A F P
Organization well planned	E G A F P
Language accurate	E G A F P
Language clear	E G A F P
Language appropriate	E G A F P
Connectives effective	E G A F P

CONCLUSION

Prepared audience for ending	E G A F P
Reinforced central idea	E G A F P
Vivid ending	E G A F P

DELIVERY

Began speech without rushing	E G A F P
Maintained strong eye contact	E G A F P
Avoided distracting mannerisms	E G A F P
Articulated words clearly	E G A F P
Used pauses effectively	E G A F P
Used vocal variety to add impact	E G A F P
Prepared visual aids well	E G A F P
Presented visual aids well	E G A F P
Communicated enthusiasm for topic	E G A F P
Departed from lectern without rushing	E G A F P

OVERALL EVALUATION

Met assignment	E G A F P
Topic challenging	E G A F P
Specific purpose well chosen	E G A F P
Message adapted to audience	E G A F P
Speech completed within time limit	E G A F P
Held interest of audience	E G A F P

_____

What did the speaker do most effectively? _____

_____

_____

What should the speaker pay special attention to next time? _____

_____

_____

General Comments: _____

_____

_____

_____

SPEECH EVALUATION FORM

Speaker _____

Topic _____

Rate the speaker on each point: *E-excellent*   *G-good*   *A-average*   *F-fair*   *P-poor*

INTRODUCTION

Gained attention and interest	E G A F P
Introduced topic clearly	E G A F P
Related topic to audience	E G A F P
Established credibility	E G A F P
Previewed body of speech	E G A F P

BODY

Main points clear	E G A F P
Main points fully supported	E G A F P
Organization well planned	E G A F P
Language accurate	E G A F P
Language clear	E G A F P
Language appropriate	E G A F P
Connectives effective	E G A F P

CONCLUSION

Prepared audience for ending	E G A F P
Reinforced central idea	E G A F P
Vivid ending	E G A F P

DELIVERY

Began speech without rushing	E G A F P
Maintained strong eye contact	E G A F P
Avoided distracting mannerisms	E G A F P
Articulated words clearly	E G A F P
Used pauses effectively	E G A F P
Used vocal variety to add impact	E G A F P
Prepared visual aids well	E G A F P
Presented visual aids well	E G A F P
Communicated enthusiasm for topic	E G A F P
Departed from lectern without rushing	E G A F P

OVERALL EVALUATION

Met assignment	E G A F P
Topic challenging	E G A F P
Specific purpose well chosen	E G A F P
Message adapted to audience	E G A F P
Speech completed within time limit	E G A F P
Held interest of audience	E G A F P

_____

What did the speaker do most effectively? _____

_____

_____

What should the speaker pay special attention to next time? _____

_____

_____

General Comments: _____

_____

_____

_____

SPEECH EVALUATION FORM

Speaker _____

Topic _____

Rate the speaker on each point: E-excellent   G-good   A-average   F-fair   P-poor

INTRODUCTION

Gained attention and interest	E G A F P
Introduced topic clearly	E G A F P
Related topic to audience	E G A F P
Established credibility	E G A F P
Previewed body of speech	E G A F P

BODY

Main points clear	E G A F P
Main points fully supported	E G A F P
Organization well planned	E G A F P
Language accurate	E G A F P
Language clear	E G A F P
Language appropriate	E G A F P
Connectives effective	E G A F P

CONCLUSION

Prepared audience for ending	E G A F P
Reinforced central idea	E G A F P
Vivid ending	E G A F P

DELIVERY

Began speech without rushing	E G A F P
Maintained strong eye contact	E G A F P
Avoided distracting mannerisms	E G A F P
Articulated words clearly	E G A F P
Used pauses effectively	E G A F P
Used vocabulary to add impact	E G A F P
Prepared visual aids well	E G A F P
Presented visual aids well	E G A F P
Communicated enthusiasm for topic	E G A F P
Departed from lectern without rushing	E G A F P

OVERALL EVALUATION

Met assignment	E G A F P
Topic challenging	E G A F P
Specific purpose well chosen	E G A F P
Message adapted to audience	E G A F P
Speech completed within time limit	E G A F P
Held interest of audience	E G A F P

What did the speaker do most effectively.
_____
_____

What should the speaker pay special attention to next time?
_____
_____

General Comments.
_____
_____
_____

SPEECH EVALUATION FORM

Speaker _____

Topic _____

Rate the speaker on each point: *E-excellent*   *G-good*   *A-average*   *F-fair*   *P-poor*

INTRODUCTION

Gained attention and interest	E G A F P
Introduced topic clearly	E G A F P
Related topic to audience	E G A F P
Established credibility	E G A F P
Previewed body of speech	E G A F P

BODY

Main points clear	E G A F P
Main points fully supported	E G A F P
Organization well planned	E G A F P
Language accurate	E G A F P
Language clear	E G A F P
Language appropriate	E G A F P
Connectives effective	E G A F P

CONCLUSION

Prepared audience for ending	E G A F P
Reinforced central idea	E G A F P
Vivid ending	E G A F P

DELIVERY

Began speech without rushing	E G A F P
Maintained strong eye contact	E G A F P
Avoided distracting mannerisms	E G A F P
Articulated words clearly	E G A F P
Used pauses effectively	E G A F P
Used vocal variety to add impact	E G A F P
Prepared visual aids well	E G A F P
Presented visual aids well	E G A F P
Communicated enthusiasm for topic	E G A F P
Departed from lectern without rushing	E G A F P

OVERALL EVALUATION

Met assignment	E G A F P
Topic challenging	E G A F P
Specific purpose well chosen	E G A F P
Message adapted to audience	E G A F P
Speech completed within time limit	E G A F P
Held interest of audience	E G A F P

_____

What did the speaker do most effectively? _____

_____

_____

What should the speaker pay special attention to next time? _____

_____

_____

General Comments: _____

_____

_____

_____

SPEECH EVALUATION FORM

Speaker

Topic

Rate the speaker on each point: Excellent Good Average Fair Poor

INTRODUCTION

	E	G	A	F	P
Gained attention and interest	E	G	A	F	P
Introduced topic clearly	E	G	A	F	P
Related topic to audience	E	G	A	F	P
Established credibility	E	G	A	F	P
Previewed body of speech	E	G	A	F	P

BODY

	E	G	A	F	P
Main points clear	E	G	A	F	P
Main points fully supported	E	G	A	F	P
Organization well planned	E	G	A	F	P
Language accurate	E	G	A	F	P
Language clear	E	G	A	F	P
Language appropriate	E	G	A	F	P
Connectives effective	E	G	A	F	P

CONCLUSION

	E	G	A	F	P
Prepared audience for ending	E	G	A	F	P
Reinforced central idea	E	G	A	F	P
Vivid ending	E	G	A	F	P

DELIVERY

	E	G	A	F	P
Began speech without rushing	E	G	A	F	P
Maintained strong eye contact	E	G	A	F	P
Avoided distracting mannerisms	E	G	A	F	P
Articulated words clearly	E	G	A	F	P
Used pauses effectively	E	G	A	F	P
Used vocal variety to add impact	E	G	A	F	P
Presented visual aids well	E	G	A	F	P
Communicated enthusiasm for topic	E	G	A	F	P
Departed from lectern without rushing	E	G	A	F	P

OVERALL EVALUATION

	E	G	A	F	P
Met assignment	E	G	A	F	P
Topic challenging	E	G	A	F	P
Specific purpose well chosen	E	G	A	F	P
Message adapted to audience	E	G	A	F	P
Speech completed within time limit	E	G	A	F	P
Held interest of audience	E	G	A	F	P

What did the speaker do most effectively?

What should the speaker pay special attention to next time?

General Comments:

SPEECH EVALUATION FORM

Speaker _____

Topic _____

Rate the speaker on each point: *E-excellent*   *G-good*   *A-average*   *F-fair*   *P-poor*

INTRODUCTION

Gained attention and interest	E G A F P
Introduced topic clearly	E G A F P
Related topic to audience	E G A F P
Established credibility	E G A F P
Previewed body of speech	E G A F P

BODY

Main points clear	E G A F P
Main points fully supported	E G A F P
Organization well planned	E G A F P
Language accurate	E G A F P
Language clear	E G A F P
Language appropriate	E G A F P
Connectives effective	E G A F P

CONCLUSION

Prepared audience for ending	E G A F P
Reinforced central idea	E G A F P
Vivid ending	E G A F P

DELIVERY

Began speech without rushing	E G A F P
Maintained strong eye contact	E G A F P
Avoided distracting mannerisms	E G A F P
Articulated words clearly	E G A F P
Used pauses effectively	E G A F P
Used vocal variety to add impact	E G A F P
Prepared visual aids well	E G A F P
Presented visual aids well	E G A F P
Communicated enthusiasm for topic	E G A F P
Departed from lectern without rushing	E G A F P

OVERALL EVALUATION

Met assignment	E G A F P
Topic challenging	E G A F P
Specific purpose well chosen	E G A F P
Message adapted to audience	E G A F P
Speech completed within time limit	E G A F P
Held interest of audience	E G A F P

_____

What did the speaker do most effectively? _____

_____

_____

What should the speaker pay special attention to next time? _____

_____

_____

General Comments: _____

_____

_____

_____

SPEECH EVALUATION FORM

Speaker _____

Topic _____

Rate the speaker on each item: E=excellent   B=good   A=average   F=fair   P=poor

INTRODUCTION

	E	B	G	A	F	P
Gained attention and interest		B	G	A	F	P
Introduced topic clearly		B	G	A	F	P
Related topic to audience		B	G	A	F	P
Established credibility		B	G	A	F	P
Previewed body of speech		B	G	A	F	P

BODY

	E	B	G	A	F	P
Main points clear		B	G	A	F	P
Main points were supported		B	G	A	F	P
Organization well planned		B	G	A	F	P
Language accurate		B	G	A	F	P
Language clear		B	G	A	F	P
Language appropriate		B	G	A	F	P
Connectives effective		B	G	A	F	P

CONCLUSION

	E	B	G	A	F	P
Prepared audience for ending		B	G	A	F	P
Reinforced central idea		B	G	A	F	P
Vivid ending		B	G	A	F	P

DELIVERY

	E	B	G	A	F	P
Began speech without rushing		B	G	A	F	P
Maintained strong eye contact		B	G	A	F	P
Avoided distracting mannerisms		B	G	A	F	P
Articulated words clearly		B	G	A	F	P
Used pauses effectively		B	G	A	F	P
Used vocal variety to add impact		B	G	A	F	P
Appeared vocally confident		B	G	A	F	P
Presented visual aids well		B	G	A	F	P
Communicated enthusiasm for topic		B	G	A	F	P
Departed from lectern without rushing		B	G	A	F	P

OVERALL EVALUATION

	E	B	G	A	F	P
Met assignment		B	G	A	F	P
Topic challenging		B	G	A	F	P
Specific purpose well chosen		B	G	A	F	P
Message adapted to audience		B	G	A	F	P
Speech completed within time limit		B	G	A	F	P
Held interest of audience		B	G	A	F	P

What did the speaker do most effectively?

What should the speaker pay special attention to next time?

General comments:

SPEECH EVALUATION FORM

Speaker _____

Topic _____

Rate the speaker on each point: *E-excellent*   *G-good*   *A-average*   *F-fair*   *P-poor*

INTRODUCTION

Gained attention and interest	E G A F P	
Introduced topic clearly	E G A F P	
Related topic to audience	E G A F P	
Established credibility	E G A F P	
Previewed body of speech	E G A F P	

BODY

Main points clear	E G A F P
Main points fully supported	E G A F P
Organization well planned	E G A F P
Language accurate	E G A F P
Language clear	E G A F P
Language appropriate	E G A F P
Connectives effective	E G A F P

CONCLUSION

Prepared audience for ending	E G A F P
Reinforced central idea	E G A F P
Vivid ending	E G A F P

DELIVERY

Began speech without rushing	E G A F P
Maintained strong eye contact	E G A F P
Avoided distracting mannerisms	E G A F P
Articulated words clearly	E G A F P
Used pauses effectively	E G A F P
Used vocal variety to add impact	E G A F P
Prepared visual aids well	E G A F P
Presented visual aids well	E G A F P
Communicated enthusiasm for topic	E G A F P
Departed from lectern without rushing	E G A F P

OVERALL EVALUATION

Met assignment	E G A F P
Topic challenging	E G A F P
Specific purpose well chosen	E G A F P
Message adapted to audience	E G A F P
Speech completed within time limit	E G A F P
Held interest of audience	E G A F P

What did the speaker do most effectively? _____

_____

_____

What should the speaker pay special attention to next time? _____

_____

_____

General Comments: _____

_____

_____

_____

SPEECH EVALUATION FORM

Speaker _____

Topic _____

Rate the speaker on each point: E-*excellent*   G-*good*   A-*average*   F-*fair*   P-*poor*

INTRODUCTION

Gained attention and interest	E G A F P
Introduced topic clearly	E G A F P
Related topic to audience	E G A F P
Established credibility	E G A F P
Previewed body of speech	E G A F P

BODY

Main points clear	E G A F P
Main points fully supported	E G A F P
Organization well planned	E G A F P
Language accurate	E G A F P
Language clear	E G A F P
Language appropriate	E G A F P
Connectives effective	E G A F P

CONCLUSION

Prepared audience for ending	E G A F P
Reinforced central idea	E G A F P
Vivid ending	E G A F P

DELIVERY

Began speech without rushing	E G A F P
Maintained strong eye contact	E G A F P
Avoided distracting mannerisms	E G A F P
Articulated words clearly	E G A F P
Used pauses effectively	E G A F P
Used vocal variety to add impact	E G A F P
Prepared visual aids well	E G A F P
Presented visual aids well	E G A F P
Communicated enthusiasm for topic	E G A F P
Departed from lectern without rushing	E G A F P

OVERALL EVALUATION

Met assignment	E G A F P
Topic challenging	E G A F P
Specific purpose well chosen	E G A F P
Message adapted to audience	E G A F P
Speech completed within time limit	E G A F P
Held interest of audience	E G A F P

_____

What did the speaker do most effectively? _____

_____

What should the speaker pay special attention to next time? _____

_____

General Comments: _____

_____

SPEECH EVALUATION FORM

Speaker _____

Topic _____

Rate the speaker on each point: E = excellent • G = good • A = average • F = fair • P = poor

INTRODUCTION

Gained attention and interest   E G A F P
Introduced topic clearly   E G A F P
Related topic to audience   E G A F P
Established credibility   E G A F P
Previewed body of speech   E G A F P

BODY

Main points clear   E G A F P
Main points fully supported   E G A F P
Organization well planned   E G A F P
Language accurate   E G A F P
Language clear   E G A F P
Language appropriate   E G A F P
Connectives effective   E G A F P

CONCLUSION

Prepared audience for ending   E G A F P
Reinforced central idea   E G A F P
Vivid ending   E G A F P

DELIVERY

Began speech without rushing   E G A F P
Maintained strong eye contact   E G A F P
Avoided distracting mannerisms   E G A F P
Articulated words clearly   E G A F P
Used pauses effectively   E G A F P
Used vocal variety to add impact   E G A F P
Prepared visual aids well   E G A F P
Presented visual aids well   E G A F P
Communicated enthusiasm for topic   E G A F P
Departed from lectern without rushing   E G A F P

OVERALL EVALUATION

Met assignment   E G A F P
Topic challenging   E G A F P
Specific purpose well chosen   E G A F P
Message adapted to audience   E G A F P
Speech completed within time limit   E G A F P
Held interest of audience   E G A F P

What did the speaker do most effectively? _____

What should the speaker pay special attention to next time? _____

General comments. _____

SPEECH EVALUATION FORM

Speaker _____

Topic _____

Rate the speaker on each point: *E-excellent*   *G-good*   *A-average*   *F-fair*   *P-poor*

INTRODUCTION

Gained attention and interest	E G A F P
Introduced topic clearly	E G A F P
Related topic to audience	E G A F P
Established credibility	E G A F P
Previewed body of speech	E G A F P

BODY

Main points clear	E G A F P
Main points fully supported	E G A F P
Organization well planned	E G A F P
Language accurate	E G A F P
Language clear	E G A F P
Language appropriate	E G A F P
Connectives effective	E G A F P

CONCLUSION

Prepared audience for ending	E G A F P
Reinforced central idea	E G A F P
Vivid ending	E G A F P

DELIVERY

Began speech without rushing	E G A F P
Maintained strong eye contact	E G A F P
Avoided distracting mannerisms	E G A F P
Articulated words clearly	E G A F P
Used pauses effectively	E G A F P
Used vocal variety to add impact	E G A F P
Prepared visual aids well	E G A F P
Presented visual aids well	E G A F P
Communicated enthusiasm for topic	E G A F P
Departed from lectern without rushing	E G A F P

OVERALL EVALUATION

Met assignment	E G A F P
Topic challenging	E G A F P
Specific purpose well chosen	E G A F P
Message adapted to audience	E G A F P
Speech completed within time limit	E G A F P
Held interest of audience	E G A F P

_____

What did the speaker do most effectively? _____

_____

_____

What should the speaker pay special attention to next time? _____

_____

_____

General Comments: _____

_____

_____

_____

SPEECH EVALUATION FORM

Speaker _____

Topic _____

Rate the speaker on each point: Excellent   Superior   Good   Average   Fair   Poor

INTRODUCTION

Gained attention and interest	E	S	G	A	F	P
Introduced topic clearly	E	S	G	A	F	P
Related topic to audience	E	S	G	A	F	P
Established credibility	E	S	G	A	F	P
Previewed body of speech	E	S	G	A	F	P

BODY

Main points clear	E	S	G	A	F	P
Main points fully supported	E	S	G	A	F	P
Organization well planned	E	S	G	A	F	P
Language accurate	E	S	G	A	F	P
Language appropriate	E	S	G	A	F	P
Connectives effective	E	S	G	A	F	P

CONCLUSION

Prepared audience for ending	E	S	G	A	F	P
Reinforced central idea	E	S	G	A	F	P
Vivid ending	E	S	G	A	F	P

DELIVERY

Began speech without rushing	E	S	G	A	F	P
Maintained strong eye contact	E	S	G	A	F	P
Avoided distracting mannerisms	E	S	G	A	F	P
Articulated words clearly	E	S	G	A	F	P
Used pauses effectively	E	S	G	A	F	P
Used vocal variety to add impact	E	S	G	A	F	P
Presented visual aids well	E	S	G	A	F	P
Communicated enthusiasm for topic	E	S	G	A	F	P
Departed from lectern without rushing	E	S	G	A	F	P

OVERALL EVALUATION

Met assignment	E	S	G	A	F	P
Topic challenging	E	S	G	A	F	P
Specific purpose well chosen	E	S	G	A	F	P
Message adapted to audience	E	S	G	A	F	P
Speech completed within time limit	E	S	G	A	F	P
Held interest of audience	E	S	G	A	F	P

What did the speaker do most effectively?

_____

_____

What should the speaker pay special attention to next time?

_____

_____

General Comments:

_____

_____

SPEECH EVALUATION FORM

Speaker _____

Topic _____

Rate the speaker on each point: *E-excellent*   *G-good*   *A-average*   *F-fair*   *P-poor*

INTRODUCTION

Gained attention and interest	E G A F P
Introduced topic clearly	E G A F P
Related topic to audience	E G A F P
Established credibility	E G A F P
Previewed body of speech	E G A F P

BODY

Main points clear	E G A F P
Main points fully supported	E G A F P
Organization well planned	E G A F P
Language accurate	E G A F P
Language clear	E G A F P
Language appropriate	E G A F P
Connectives effective	E G A F P

CONCLUSION

Prepared audience for ending	E G A F P
Reinforced central idea	E G A F P
Vivid ending	E G A F P

DELIVERY

Began speech without rushing	E G A F P
Maintained strong eye contact	E G A F P
Avoided distracting mannerisms	E G A F P
Articulated words clearly	E G A F P
Used pauses effectively	E G A F P
Used vocal variety to add impact	E G A F P
Prepared visual aids well	E G A F P
Presented visual aids well	E G A F P
Communicated enthusiasm for topic	E G A F P
Departed from lectern without rushing	E G A F P

OVERALL EVALUATION

Met assignment	E G A F P
Topic challenging	E G A F P
Specific purpose well chosen	E G A F P
Message adapted to audience	E G A F P
Speech completed within time limit	E G A F P
Held interest of audience	E G A F P

_____

What did the speaker do most effectively? _____

_____

_____

What should the speaker pay special attention to next time? _____

_____

_____

General Comments: _____

_____

_____

_____

SPEECH EVALUATION FORM

Speaker _____

Topic _____

Rate the speaker in each point: E-excellent   G-good   A-average   F-fair   P-poor

INTRODUCTION

Gained attention and interest   E G A F P
Introduced topic clearly   E G A F P
Related topic to audience   E G A F P
Established credibility   E G A F P
Previewed body of speech   E G A F P

BODY

Main points clear   E G A F P
Main points fully supported   E G A F P
Organization well planned   E G A F P
Language accurate   E G A F P
Language clear   E G A F P
Language appropriate   E G A F P
Connectives effective   E G A F P

CONCLUSION

Prepared audience for ending   E G A F P
Reinforced central idea   E G A F P
Vivid ending   E G A F P

DELIVERY

Began speech without reading   E G A F P
Maintained strong eye contact   E G A F P
Avoided distracting mannerisms   E G A F P
Articulated words clearly   E G A F P
Used pauses effectively   E G A F P
Used vocal variety to add impact   E G A F P
Prepared visual aids well   E G A F P
Presented visual aids well   E G A F P
Communicated enthusiasm for topic   E G A F P
Departed from lectern without rushing   E G A F P

OVERALL EVALUATION

Met assignment   E G A F P
Topic challenging   E G A F P
Specific purpose well chosen   E G A F P
Message adapted to audience   E G A F P
Speech completed within time limit   E G A F P
Held interest of audience   E G A F P

What did the speaker do most effectively? _____

_____

What should the speaker pay special attention to next time? _____

_____

General Comments: _____

_____

SPEECH EVALUATION FORM

Speaker _____

Topic _____

Rate the speaker on each point: E-excellent   G-good   A-average   F-fair   P-poor

INTRODUCTION

Gained attention and interest	E G A F P
Introduced topic clearly	E G A F P
Related topic to audience	E G A F P
Established credibility	E G A F P
Previewed body of speech	E G A F P

BODY

Main points clear	E G A F P
Main points fully supported	E G A F P
Organization well planned	E G A F P
Language accurate	E G A F P
Language clear	E G A F P
Language appropriate	E G A F P
Connectives effective	E G A F P

CONCLUSION

Prepared audience for ending	E G A F P
Reinforced central idea	E G A F P
Vivid ending	E G A F P

DELIVERY

Began speech without rushing	E G A F P
Maintained strong eye contact	E G A F P
Avoided distracting mannerisms	E G A F P
Articulated words clearly	E G A F P
Used pauses effectively	E G A F P
Used vocal variety to add impact	E G A F P
Prepared visual aids well	E G A F P
Presented visual aids well	E G A F P
Communicated enthusiasm for topic	E G A F P
Departed from lectern without rushing	E G A F P

OVERALL EVALUATION

Met assignment	E G A F P
Topic challenging	E G A F P
Specific purpose well chosen	E G A F P
Message adapted to audience	E G A F P
Speech completed within time limit	E G A F P
Held interest of audience	E G A F P

_____

What did the speaker do most effectively? _____

_____

_____

What should the speaker pay special attention to next time? _____

_____

_____

General Comments: _____

_____

_____

_____

SPEECH EVALUATION FORM

Speaker _____

Topic _____

Rate the speaker on each point: *E-excellent*   *G-good*   *A-average*   *F-fair*   *P-poor*

INTRODUCTION

Gained attention and interest	E G A F P
Introduced topic clearly	E G A F P
Related topic to audience	E G A F P
Established credibility	E G A F P
Previewed body of speech	E G A F P

BODY

Main points clear	E G A F P
Main points fully supported	E G A F P
Organization well planned	E G A F P
Language accurate	E G A F P
Language clear	E G A F P
Language appropriate	E G A F P
Connectives effective	E G A F P

CONCLUSION

Prepared audience for ending	E G A F P
Reinforced central idea	E G A F P
Vivid ending	E G A F P

DELIVERY

Began speech without rushing	E G A F P
Maintained strong eye contact	E G A F P
Avoided distracting mannerisms	E G A F P
Articulated words clearly	E G A F P
Used pauses effectively	E G A F P
Used vocal variety to add impact	E G A F P
Prepared visual aids well	E G A F P
Presented visual aids well	E G A F P
Communicated enthusiasm for topic	E G A F P
Departed from lectern without rushing	E G A F P

OVERALL EVALUATION

Met assignment	E G A F P
Topic challenging	E G A F P
Specific purpose well chosen	E G A F P
Message adapted to audience	E G A F P
Speech completed within time limit	E G A F P
Held interest of audience	E G A F P

_____

What did the speaker do most effectively? _____

_____

_____

What should the speaker pay special attention to next time? _____

_____

_____

General Comments: _____

_____

_____

_____

SPEECH EVALUATION FORM

Speaker _____

Topic _____

Rate the speaker on each point: E-excellent   G-good   A-average   F-fair   P-poor

INTRODUCTION

Gained attention and interest	E	G	A	F	P
Introduced topic clearly	E	G	A	F	P
Related topic to audience	E	G	A	F	P
Established credibility	E	G	A	F	P
Previewed body of speech	E	G	A	F	P

BODY

Main points clear	E	G	A	F	P
Main points fully supported	E	G	A	F	P
Organization well planned	E	G	A	F	P
Language accurate	E	G	A	F	P
Language clear	E	G	A	F	P
Language appropriate	E	G	A	F	P
Connectives effective	E	G	A	F	P

CONCLUSION

Prepared audience for ending	E	G	A	F	P
Reinforced central idea	E	G	A	F	P
Vivid ending	E	G	A	F	P

DELIVERY

Began speech without rushing	E	G	A	F	P
Maintained strong eye contact	E	G	A	F	P
Avoided distracting mannerisms	E	G	A	F	P
Articulated words clearly	E	G	A	F	P
Used pauses effectively	E	G	A	F	P
Used vocal variety to add impact	E	G	A	F	P
Prepared visual aids well	E	G	A	F	P
Presented visual aids well	E	G	A	F	P
Communicated enthusiasm for topic	E	G	A	F	P
Departed from lectern without rushing	E	G	A	F	P

OVERALL EVALUATION

Met assignment	E	G	A	F	P
Topic challenging	E	G	A	F	P
Specific purpose well chosen	E	G	A	F	P
Message adapted to audience	E	G	A	F	P
Speech completed within time limit	E	G	A	F	P
Held interest of audience	E	G	A	F	P

What did the speaker do most effectively? _____

_____

_____

What should the speaker pay special attention to next time? _____

_____

_____

General Comments: _____

_____

_____

_____

SPEECH EVALUATION FORM

Speaker _____

Topic _____

Rate the speaker on each point: *E-excellent*   *G-good*   *A-average*   *F-fair*   *P-poor*

INTRODUCTION

Gained attention and interest	E G A F P
Introduced topic clearly	E G A F P
Related topic to audience	E G A F P
Established credibility	E G A F P
Previewed body of speech	E G A F P

BODY

Main points clear	E G A F P
Main points fully supported	E G A F P
Organization well planned	E G A F P
Language accurate	E G A F P
Language clear	E G A F P
Language appropriate	E G A F P
Connectives effective	E G A F P

CONCLUSION

Prepared audience for ending	E G A F P
Reinforced central idea	E G A F P
Vivid ending	E G A F P

DELIVERY

Began speech without rushing	E G A F P
Maintained strong eye contact	E G A F P
Avoided distracting mannerisms	E G A F P
Articulated words clearly	E G A F P
Used pauses effectively	E G A F P
Used vocal variety to add impact	E G A F P
Prepared visual aids well	E G A F P
Presented visual aids well	E G A F P
Communicated enthusiasm for topic	E G A F P
Departed from lectern without rushing	E G A F P

OVERALL EVALUATION

Met assignment	E G A F P
Topic challenging	E G A F P
Specific purpose well chosen	E G A F P
Message adapted to audience	E G A F P
Speech completed within time limit	E G A F P
Held interest of audience	E G A F P

_____

What did the speaker do most effectively? _____

_____

_____

What should the speaker pay special attention to next time? _____

_____

_____

_____

General Comments: _____

_____

_____

_____

SPEECH EVALUATION FORM

Speaker _____

Topic _____

Rate the speaker on each quality: E—excellent   G—good   A—average   F—fair   P—poor

INTRODUCTION

Captured attention and interest	E G A F P
Introduced topic clearly	E G A F P
Related topic to audience	E G A F P
Established rapport	E G A F P
Previewed rest of speech	E G A F P

BODY

Main points clear	E G A F P
Main points fully supported	E G A F P
Organization well planned	E G A F P
Language accurate	E G A F P
Language clear	E G A F P
Enough signposts	E G A F P
Connectives effective	E G A F P

CONCLUSION

Prepared audience for ending	E G A F P
Reinforced central idea	E G A F P
Vivid ending	E G A F P

DELIVERY

Began speech without rushing	E G A F P
Maintained strong eye contact	E G A F P
Avoided distracting mannerisms	E G A F P
Articulated words clearly	E G A F P
Used pauses effectively	E G A F P
Used vocal variety to add impact	E G A F P
Presented visual aids well	E G A F P
Presented clear and fluently	E G A F P
Communicated during Q&A	E G A F P
Departed from lectern without rushing	E G A F P

OVERALL EVALUATION

Met assignment	E G A F P
Topic challenging	E G A F P
Specific purpose well chosen	E G A F P
Message adapted to audience	E G A F P
Speech completed within time limit	E G A F P
Held interest of audience	E G A F P

What did the speaker do most effectively? _____

What should the speaker give special attention to next time? _____

General comments: _____

SPEECH EVALUATION FORM

Speaker _____

Topic _____

Rate the speaker on each point: *E-excellent*   *G-good*   *A-average*   *F-fair*   *P-poor*

INTRODUCTION

Gained attention and interest	E G A F P
Introduced topic clearly	E G A F P
Related topic to audience	E G A F P
Established credibility	E G A F P
Previewed body of speech	E G A F P

BODY

Main points clear	E G A F P
Main points fully supported	E G A F P
Organization well planned	E G A F P
Language accurate	E G A F P
Language clear	E G A F P
Language appropriate	E G A F P
Connectives effective	E G A F P

CONCLUSION

Prepared audience for ending	E G A F P
Reinforced central idea	E G A F P
Vivid ending	E G A F P

DELIVERY

Began speech without rushing	E G A F P
Maintained strong eye contact	E G A F P
Avoided distracting mannerisms	E G A F P
Articulated words clearly	E G A F P
Used pauses effectively	E G A F P
Used vocal variety to add impact	E G A F P
Prepared visual aids well	E G A F P
Presented visual aids well	E G A F P
Communicated enthusiasm for topic	E G A F P
Departed from lectern without rushing	E G A F P

OVERALL EVALUATION

Met assignment	E G A F P
Topic challenging	E G A F P
Specific purpose well chosen	E G A F P
Message adapted to audience	E G A F P
Speech completed within time limit	E G A F P
Held interest of audience	E G A F P

_____

What did the speaker do most effectively? _____

_____

_____

What should the speaker pay special attention to next time? _____

_____

_____

General Comments: _____

_____

_____

_____

SPEECH EVALUATION FORM

Speaker _____

Topic _____

Rate the speaker on each point: E=excellent   G=good   A=average   F=fair   P=poor

INTRODUCTION

Gained attention and interest		E G A F P
Introduced topic clearly		E G A F P
Related topic to audience		E G A F P
Established credibility		E G A F P
Previewed body of speech		E G A F P

BODY

Main points clear		E G A F P
Main points fully supported		E G A F P
Organization well planned		E G A F P
Language accurate		E G A F P
Language appropriate		E G A F P
Connectives effective		E G A F P

CONCLUSION

Prepared audience for ending		E G A F P
Reinforced central idea		E G A F P
Vivid ending		E G A F P

DELIVERY

Began speech without rushing		E G A F P
Maintained strong eye contact		E G A F P
Avoided distracting mannerisms		E G A F P
Articulated words clearly		E G A F P
Used pauses effectively		E G A F P
Used vocal variety to add impact		E G A F P
Presented visual aids well		E G A F P
Presented visual aid well		E G A F P
Communicated enthusiasm for topic		E G A F P
Departed from lectern without rushing		E G A F P

OVERALL EVALUATION

Met assignment		E G A F P
Topic challenging		E G A F P
Specific purpose well chosen		E G A F P
Message adapted to audience		E G A F P
Speech completed within time limit		E G A F P
Held interest of audience		E G A F P

What did the speaker do most effectively? _____

What should the speaker pay special attention to next time? _____

General Comments _____

SPEECH EVALUATION FORM

Speaker _____

Topic _____

Rate the speaker on each point: *E-excellent   G-good   A-average   F-fair   P-poor*

INTRODUCTION

Gained attention and interest   E G A F P

Introduced topic clearly   E G A F P

Related topic to audience   E G A F P

Established credibility   E G A F P

Previewed body of speech   E G A F P

BODY

Main points clear   E G A F P

Main points fully supported   E G A F P

Organization well planned   E G A F P

Language accurate   E G A F P

Language clear   E G A F P

Language appropriate   E G A F P

Connectives effective   E G A F P

CONCLUSION

Prepared audience for ending   E G A F P

Reinforced central idea   E G A F P

Vivid ending   E G A F P

DELIVERY

Began speech without rushing   E G A F P

Maintained strong eye contact   E G A F P

Avoided distracting mannerisms   E G A F P

Articulated words clearly   E G A F P

Used pauses effectively   E G A F P

Used vocal variety to add impact   E G A F P

Prepared visual aids well   E G A F P

Presented visual aids well   E G A F P

Communicated enthusiasm for topic   E G A F P

Departed from lectern without rushing   E G A F P

OVERALL EVALUATION

Met assignment   E G A F P

Topic challenging   E G A F P

Specific purpose well chosen   E G A F P

Message adapted to audience   E G A F P

Speech completed within time limit   E G A F P

Held interest of audience   E G A F P

_____

What did the speaker do most effectively? _____

_____

_____

What should the speaker pay special attention to next time? _____

_____

_____

General Comments: _____

_____

_____

_____

SPEECH EVALUATION FORM

Speaker _____

Topic _____

Rate the speaker on each point: *E-excellent*   *G-good*   *A-average*   *F-fair*   *P-poor*

INTRODUCTION

Gained attention and interest	E G A F P
Introduced topic clearly	E G A F P
Related topic to audience	E G A F P
Established credibility	E G A F P
Previewed body of speech	E G A F P

BODY

Main points clear	E G A F P
Main points fully supported	E G A F P
Organization well planned	E G A F P
Language accurate	E G A F P
Language clear	E G A F P
Language appropriate	E G A F P
Connectives effective	E G A F P

CONCLUSION

Prepared audience for ending	E G A F P
Reinforced central idea	E G A F P
Vivid ending	E G A F P

DELIVERY

Began speech without rushing	E G A F P
Maintained strong eye contact	E G A F P
Avoided distracting mannerisms	E G A F P
Articulated words clearly	E G A F P
Used pauses effectively	E G A F P
Used vocal variety to add impact	E G A F P
Prepared visual aids well	E G A F P
Presented visual aids well	E G A F P
Communicated enthusiasm for topic	E G A F P
Departed from lectern without rushing	E G A F P

OVERALL EVALUATION

Met assignment	E G A F P
Topic challenging	E G A F P
Specific purpose well chosen	E G A F P
Message adapted to audience	E G A F P
Speech completed within time limit	E G A F P
Held interest of audience	E G A F P

_____

What did the speaker do most effectively? _____

_____

_____

What should the speaker pay special attention to next time? _____

_____

_____

General Comments: _____

_____

_____

_____

SPEECH EVALUATION FORM

Speaker: _____

Topic: _____

Rate the speaker on each point: E-excellent   G-good   A-average   F-fair   P-poor

INTRODUCTION

Gained attention and interest	E G A F P
Introduced topic clearly	E G A F P
Related topic to audience	E G A F P
Established credibility	E G A F P
Previewed body of speech	E G A F P

BODY

Main point clear	E G A F P
Main points fully supported	E G A F P
Organization well planned	E G A F P
Language accurate	E G A F P
Language clear	E G A F P
Language appropriate	E G A F P
Connectives effective	E G A F P

CONCLUSION

Prepared audience for ending	E G A F P
Reinforced central idea	E G A F P
Vivid ending	E G A F P

DELIVERY

Began speech without rushing	E G A F P
Maintained strong eye contact	E G A F P
Avoided distracting mannerisms	E G A F P
Articulated words clearly	E G A F P
Used pauses effectively	E G A F P
Used vocal variety to add impact	E G A F P
Prepared visual aids well	E G A F P
Presented visual aids well	E G A F P
Communicated enthusiasm for topic	E G A F P
Departed from lectern without rushing	E G A F P

OVERALL EVALUATION

Met assignment	E G A F P
Topic challenging	E G A F P
Specific purpose well chosen	E G A F P
Message adapted to audience	E G A F P
Speech completed within time limit	E G A F P
Held interest of audience	E G A F P

What did the speaker do most effectively? _____

What should the speaker pay special attention to next time? _____

General Comments: _____

SPEECH EVALUATION FORM

Speaker _____

Topic _____

Rate the speaker on each point: *E-excellent*   *G-good*   *A-average*   *F-fair*   *P-poor*

INTRODUCTION

Gained attention and interest	E G A F P
Introduced topic clearly	E G A F P
Related topic to audience	E G A F P
Established credibility	E G A F P
Previewed body of speech	E G A F P

BODY

Main points clear	E G A F P
Main points fully supported	E G A F P
Organization well planned	E G A F P
Language accurate	E G A F P
Language clear	E G A F P
Language appropriate	E G A F P
Connectives effective	E G A F P

CONCLUSION

Prepared audience for ending	E G A F P
Reinforced central idea	E G A F P
Vivid ending	E G A F P

DELIVERY

Began speech without rushing	E G A F P
Maintained strong eye contact	E G A F P
Avoided distracting mannerisms	E G A F P
Articulated words clearly	E G A F P
Used pauses effectively	E G A F P
Used vocal variety to add impact	E G A F P
Prepared visual aids well	E G A F P
Presented visual aids well	E G A F P
Communicated enthusiasm for topic	E G A F P
Departed from lectern without rushing	E G A F P

OVERALL EVALUATION

Met assignment	E G A F P
Topic challenging	E G A F P
Specific purpose well chosen	E G A F P
Message adapted to audience	E G A F P
Speech completed within time limit	E G A F P
Held interest of audience	E G A F P

_____

What did the speaker do most effectively? _____

_____

_____

What should the speaker pay special attention to next time? _____

_____

_____

General Comments: _____

_____

_____

_____

SPEECH EVALUATION FORM

Speaker _____

Topic _____

Rate the speaker on each point: 5 excellent   4 good   3 average   2 fair   1 poor

INTRODUCTION

Gained attention and interest	5	4	3	2	1
Spoke clearly	5	4	3	2	1
Related topic to audience	5	4	3	2	1
Established credibility	5	4	3	2	1
Previewed body of speech	5	4	3	2	1

BODY

Main points clear	5	4	3	2	1
Main points fully supported	5	4	3	2	1
Organization well planned	5	4	3	2	1
Language accurate	5	4	3	2	1
Language clear	5	4	3	2	1
Language appropriate	5	4	3	2	1
Connectives effective	5	4	3	2	1

CONCLUSION

Prepared audience for ending	5	4	3	2	1
Reinforced central idea	5	4	3	2	1
Vivid ending	5	4	3	2	1

DELIVERY

Began speech without rushing	5	4	3	2	1
Maintained strong eye contact	5	4	3	2	1
Avoided distracting mannerisms	5	4	3	2	1
Articulated words clearly	5	4	3	2	1
Used pauses effectively	5	4	3	2	1
Used vocal variety to add impact	5	4	3	2	1
Presented visual aids well	5	4	3	2	1
Departed from lectern without rushing	5	4	3	2	1

OVERALL EVALUATION

Topic challenging	5	4	3	2	1
Specific purpose well chosen	5	4	3	2	1
Message adapted to audience	5	4	3	2	1
Speech completed within time limit	5	4	3	2	1
Held interest of audience	5	4	3	2	1

What did the speaker do most effectively? _____

_____

_____

What should the speaker pay special attention to next time? _____

_____

_____

General comments _____

_____

SPEECH EVALUATION FORM

Speaker _____

Topic _____

Rate the speaker on each point: *E-excellent*   *G-good*   *A-average*   *F-fair*   *P-poor*

INTRODUCTION

Gained attention and interest	E G A F P
Introduced topic clearly	E G A F P
Related topic to audience	E G A F P
Established credibility	E G A F P
Previewed body of speech	E G A F P

BODY

Main points clear	E G A F P
Main points fully supported	E G A F P
Organization well planned	E G A F P
Language accurate	E G A F P
Language clear	E G A F P
Language appropriate	E G A F P
Connectives effective	E G A F P

CONCLUSION

Prepared audience for ending	E G A F P
Reinforced central idea	E G A F P
Vivid ending	E G A F P

DELIVERY

Began speech without rushing	E G A F P
Maintained strong eye contact	E G A F P
Avoided distracting mannerisms	E G A F P
Articulated words clearly	E G A F P
Used pauses effectively	E G A F P
Used vocal variety to add impact	E G A F P
Prepared visual aids well	E G A F P
Presented visual aids well	E G A F P
Communicated enthusiasm for topic	E G A F P
Departed from lectern without rushing	E G A F P

OVERALL EVALUATION

Met assignment	E G A F P
Topic challenging	E G A F P
Specific purpose well chosen	E G A F P
Message adapted to audience	E G A F P
Speech completed within time limit	E G A F P
Held interest of audience	E G A F P

_____

What did the speaker do most effectively? _____

_____

_____

What should the speaker pay special attention to next time? _____

_____

_____

General Comments: _____

_____

_____

_____

SPEECH EVALUATION FORM

Speaker _____

Topic _____

Rate the speaker on each point: E = excellent   G = Good   A = Average   F = Fair   P = Poor

INTRODUCTION

Gained attention and interest	E	G	A	F	P
Introduced topic clearly	E	G	A	F	P
Related topic to audience	E	G	A	F	P
Established credibility	E	G	A	F	P
Previewed body of speech	E	G	A	F	P

BODY

Main points clear	E	G	A	F	P
Main points fully supported	E	G	A	F	P
Organization well planned	E	G	A	F	P
Language accurate	E	G	A	F	P
Language clear	E	G	A	F	P
Language appropriate	E	G	A	F	P
Connectives effective	E	G	A	F	P

CONCLUSION

Prepared audience for ending	E	G	A	F	P
Reinforced central idea	E	G	A	F	P
Vivid ending	E	G	A	F	P

DELIVERY

Began speech without rushing	E	G	A	F	P
Maintained strong eye contact	E	G	A	F	P
Avoided distracting mannerisms	E	G	A	F	P
Articulated words clearly	E	G	A	F	P
Used pauses effectively	E	G	A	F	P
Used vocal variety to add impact	E	G	A	F	P
Prepared visual aids well	E	G	A	F	P
Presented visual aids well	E	G	A	F	P
Communicated enthusiasm for topic	E	G	A	F	P
Departed from lectern without rushing	E	G	A	F	P

OVERALL EVALUATION

Met assignment	E	G	A	F	P
Topic challenging	E	G	A	F	P
Specific purpose well chosen	E	G	A	F	P
Message adapted to audience	E	G	A	F	P
Speech completed within time limit	E	G	A	F	P
Held interest of audience	E	G	A	F	P

What did the speaker do most effectively? _____

What should the speaker pay special attention to next time? _____

General Comments _____

SPEECH EVALUATION FORM

Speaker _____

Topic _____

Rate the speaker on each point: *E-excellent*   *G-good*   *A-average*   *F-fair*   *P-poor*

INTRODUCTION

Gained attention and interest	E G A F P
Introduced topic clearly	E G A F P
Related topic to audience	E G A F P
Established credibility	E G A F P
Previewed body of speech	E G A F P

BODY

Main points clear	E G A F P
Main points fully supported	E G A F P
Organization well planned	E G A F P
Language accurate	E G A F P
Language clear	E G A F P
Language appropriate	E G A F P
Connectives effective	E G A F P

CONCLUSION

Prepared audience for ending	E G A F P
Reinforced central idea	E G A F P
Vivid ending	E G A F P

DELIVERY

Began speech without rushing	E G A F P
Maintained strong eye contact	E G A F P
Avoided distracting mannerisms	E G A F P
Articulated words clearly	E G A F P
Used pauses effectively	E G A F P
Used vocal variety to add impact	E G A F P
Prepared visual aids well	E G A F P
Presented visual aids well	E G A F P
Communicated enthusiasm for topic	E G A F P
Departed from lectern without rushing	E G A F P

OVERALL EVALUATION

Met assignment	E G A F P
Topic challenging	E G A F P
Specific purpose well chosen	E G A F P
Message adapted to audience	E G A F P
Speech completed within time limit	E G A F P
Held interest of audience	E G A F P

_____

What did the speaker do most effectively? _____

_____

_____

What should the speaker pay special attention to next time? _____

_____

_____

General Comments: _____

_____

_____

_____

SPEECH EVALUATION FORM

Speaker _____

Topic _____

Rate the speaker on each point: *E-excellent*   *G-good*   *A-average*   *F-fair*   *P-poor*

INTRODUCTION

Gained attention and interest	E G A F P
Introduced topic clearly	E G A F P
Related topic to audience	E G A F P
Established credibility	E G A F P
Previewed body of speech	E G A F P

BODY

Main points clear	E G A F P
Main points fully supported	E G A F P
Organization well planned	E G A F P
Language accurate	E G A F P
Language clear	E G A F P
Language appropriate	E G A F P
Connectives effective	E G A F P

CONCLUSION

Prepared audience for ending	E G A F P
Reinforced central idea	E G A F P
Vivid ending	E G A F P

DELIVERY

Began speech without rushing	E G A F P
Maintained strong eye contact	E G A F P
Avoided distracting mannerisms	E G A F P
Articulated words clearly	E G A F P
Used pauses effectively	E G A F P
Used vocal variety to add impact	E G A F P
Prepared visual aids well	E G A F P
Presented visual aids well	E G A F P
Communicated enthusiasm for topic	E G A F P
Departed from lectern without rushing	E G A F P

OVERALL EVALUATION

Met assignment	E G A F P
Topic challenging	E G A F P
Specific purpose well chosen	E G A F P
Message adapted to audience	E G A F P
Speech completed within time limit	E G A F P
Held interest of audience	E G A F P

_____

What did the speaker do most effectively? _____

_____

_____

What should the speaker pay special attention to next time? _____

_____

_____

General Comments: _____

_____

_____

_____

SPEECH EVALUATION FORM

Speaker _____

Topic _____

Rate the speaker on each point: E-excellent   G-good   A-average   F-fair   P-poor

INTRODUCTION

Gained attention and interest		E G A F P
Introduced topic clearly		E G A F P
Related topic to audience		E G A F P
Enhanced credibility		E G A F P
Previewed body of speech		E G A F P

BODY

Main points clear		E G A F P
Main points fully supported		E G A F P
Organization well planned		E G A F P
Language accurate		E G A F P
Language clear		E G A F P
Language appropriate		E G A F P
Connectives effective		E G A F P

CONCLUSION

Prepared audience for ending		E G A F P
Reinforced central idea		E G A F P
Vivid ending		E G A F P

DELIVERY

Began speech without rushing		E G A F P
Maintained strong eye contact		E G A F P
Avoided distracting mannerisms		E G A F P
Articulated words clearly		E G A F P
Used pauses effectively		E G A F P
Used vocal variety to add impact		E G A F P
Presented visual aids well		E G A F P
Communicated enthusiasm for topic		E G A F P
Departed from lectern without rushing		E G A F P

OVERALL EVALUATION

Met assignment		E G A F P
Topic challenging		E G A F P
Specific purpose well chosen		E G A F P
Message adapted to audience		E G A F P
Speech completed within time limit		E G A F P
Held interest of audience		E G A F P

What did the speaker do most effectively? _____

_____

_____

What should the speaker pay special attention to next time? _____

_____

_____

General Comments: _____

_____

_____

SPEECH EVALUATION FORM

Speaker _____

Topic _____

Rate the speaker on each point: *E-excellent*   *G-good*   *A-average*   *F-fair*   *P-poor*

INTRODUCTION

Gained attention and interest	E G A F P
Introduced topic clearly	E G A F P
Related topic to audience	E G A F P
Established credibility	E G A F P
Previewed body of speech	E G A F P

BODY

Main points clear	E G A F P
Main points fully supported	E G A F P
Organization well planned	E G A F P
Language accurate	E G A F P
Language clear	E G A F P
Language appropriate	E G A F P
Connectives effective	E G A F P

CONCLUSION

Prepared audience for ending	E G A F P
Reinforced central idea	E G A F P
Vivid ending	E G A F P

DELIVERY

Began speech without rushing	E G A F P
Maintained strong eye contact	E G A F P
Avoided distracting mannerisms	E G A F P
Articulated words clearly	E G A F P
Used pauses effectively	E G A F P
Used vocal variety to add impact	E G A F P
Prepared visual aids well	E G A F P
Presented visual aids well	E G A F P
Communicated enthusiasm for topic	E G A F P
Departed from lectern without rushing	E G A F P

OVERALL EVALUATION

Met assignment	E G A F P
Topic challenging	E G A F P
Specific purpose well chosen	E G A F P
Message adapted to audience	E G A F P
Speech completed within time limit	E G A F P
Held interest of audience	E G A F P

_____

What did the speaker do most effectively? _____

_____

_____

What should the speaker pay special attention to next time? _____

_____

_____

General Comments: _____

_____

_____

_____

SPEECH EVALUATION FORM

Speaker: _____

Topic: _____

Rate the speaker on each point: E Excellent   G Good   A Average   F Fair   P Poor

INTRODUCTION

Gained attention and interest	E G A F P
Introduced topic clearly	E G A F P
Related topic to audience	E G A F P
Established credibility	E G A F P
Previewed body of speech	E G A F P

BODY

Main points clear	E G A F P
Main points supported	E G A F P
Organization well planned	E G A F P
Language accurate	E G A F P
Language clear	E G A F P
Language appropriate	E G A F P
Connectives effective	E G A F P

CONCLUSION

Prepared audience for ending	E G A F P
Reinforced central idea	E G A F P
Vivid ending	E G A F P

DELIVERY

Began speech without rushing	E G A F P
Maintained strong eye contact	E G A F P
Avoided distracting mannerisms	E G A F P
Articulated words clearly	E G A F P
Used pauses effectively	E G A F P
Used vocal variety to add impact	E G A F P
Pronounced words well	E G A F P
Presented visual aids well	E G A F P
Communicated enthusiasm for topic	E G A F P
Departed from lectern without rushing	E G A F P

OVERALL EVALUATION

Met assignment	E G A F P
Topic challenging	E G A F P
Specific purpose well chosen	E G A F P
Message adapted to audience	E G A F P
Speech completed within time limit	E G A F P
Held interest of audience	E G A F P

What did the speaker do most effectively?

_____

_____

What should the speaker pay special attention to next time?

_____

_____

General Comments

_____

_____

_____

SPEECH EVALUATION FORM

Speaker _____

Topic _____

Rate the speaker on each point: *E-excellent*   *G-good*   *A-average*   *F-fair*   *P-poor*

INTRODUCTION

Gained attention and interest	E G A F P
Introduced topic clearly	E G A F P
Related topic to audience	E G A F P
Established credibility	E G A F P
Previewed body of speech	E G A F P

BODY

Main points clear	E G A F P
Main points fully supported	E G A F P
Organization well planned	E G A F P
Language accurate	E G A F P
Language clear	E G A F P
Language appropriate	E G A F P
Connectives effective	E G A F P

CONCLUSION

Prepared audience for ending	E G A F P
Reinforced central idea	E G A F P
Vivid ending	E G A F P

DELIVERY

Began speech without rushing	E G A F P
Maintained strong eye contact	E G A F P
Avoided distracting mannerisms	E G A F P
Articulated words clearly	E G A F P
Used pauses effectively	E G A F P
Used vocal variety to add impact	E G A F P
Prepared visual aids well	E G A F P
Presented visual aids well	E G A F P
Communicated enthusiasm for topic	E G A F P
Departed from lectern without rushing	E G A F P

OVERALL EVALUATION

Met assignment	E G A F P
Topic challenging	E G A F P
Specific purpose well chosen	E G A F P
Message adapted to audience	E G A F P
Speech completed within time limit	E G A F P
Held interest of audience	E G A F P

_____

What did the speaker do most effectively? _____

_____

What should the speaker pay special attention to next time? _____

_____

General Comments: _____

_____

_____

_____

SPEECH EVALUATION FORM

Speaker

Topic

Rate the speaker on each point: Outstanding   Good   Average   Fair   Poor

INTRODUCTION

Gained attention and interest	E	G	A	F	P
Introduced topic clearly	E	G	A	F	P
Related topic to audience	E	G	A	F	P
Established credibility	E	G	A	F	P
Previewed body of speech	E	G	A	F	P

BODY

Main points clear	E	G	A	F	P
Main points fully supported	E	G	A	F	P
Organization well planned	E	G	A	F	P
Language accurate	E	G	A	F	P
Language clear	E	G	A	F	P
Language appropriate	E	G	A	F	P
Connectives effective	E	G	A	F	P

CONCLUSION

Prepared audience for ending	E	G	A	F	P
Reinforced central idea	E	G	A	F	P
Vivid ending	E	G	A	F	P

DELIVERY

Began speech without rushing	E	G	A	F	P
Maintained strong eye contact	E	G	A	F	P
Avoided distracting mannerisms	E	G	A	F	P
Articulated words clearly	E	G	A	F	P
Used pauses effectively	E	G	A	F	P
Used vocal variety to add impact	E	G	A	F	P
Prepared visual aids well	E	G	A	F	P
Presented visual aids well	E	G	A	F	P
Communicated enthusiasm for topic	E	G	A	F	P
Departed from lectern without rushing	E	G	A	F	P

OVERALL EVALUATION

Message clear	E	G	A	F	P
Topic challenging	E	G	A	F	P
Specific purpose well chosen	E	G	A	F	P
Message adapted to audience	E	G	A	F	P
Speech completed within time limit	E	G	A	F	P
Held interest of audience	E	G	A	F	P

What did the speaker do most effectively?

What should the speaker pay special attention to next time?

General Comments:

SPEECH EVALUATION FORM

Speaker _____

Topic _____

Rate the speaker on each point: *E-excellent*   *G-good*   *A-average*   *F-fair*   *P-poor*

INTRODUCTION

Gained attention and interest	E G A F P
Introduced topic clearly	E G A F P
Related topic to audience	E G A F P
Established credibility	E G A F P
Previewed body of speech	E G A F P

BODY

Main points clear	E G A F P
Main points fully supported	E G A F P
Organization well planned	E G A F P
Language accurate	E G A F P
Language clear	E G A F P
Language appropriate	E G A F P
Connectives effective	E G A F P

CONCLUSION

Prepared audience for ending	E G A F P
Reinforced central idea	E G A F P
Vivid ending	E G A F P

DELIVERY

Began speech without rushing	E G A F P
Maintained strong eye contact	E G A F P
Avoided distracting mannerisms	E G A F P
Articulated words clearly	E G A F P
Used pauses effectively	E G A F P
Used vocal variety to add impact	E G A F P
Prepared visual aids well	E G A F P
Presented visual aids well	E G A F P
Communicated enthusiasm for topic	E G A F P
Departed from lectern without rushing	E G A F P

OVERALL EVALUATION

Met assignment	E G A F P
Topic challenging	E G A F P
Specific purpose well chosen	E G A F P
Message adapted to audience	E G A F P
Speech completed within time limit	E G A F P
Held interest of audience	E G A F P

_____

What did the speaker do most effectively? _____

_____

_____

What should the speaker pay special attention to next time? _____

_____

_____

General Comments: _____

_____

_____

_____

SPEECH EVALUATION FORM

Speaker _____

Topic _____

Rate the speaker on each point: *E-excellent*   *G-good*   *A-average*   *F-fair*   *P-poor*

INTRODUCTION

Gained attention and interest	E G A F P
Introduced topic clearly	E G A F P
Related topic to audience	E G A F P
Established credibility	E G A F P
Previewed body of speech	E G A F P

BODY

Main points clear	E G A F P
Main points fully supported	E G A F P
Organization well planned	E G A F P
Language accurate	E G A F P
Language clear	E G A F P
Language appropriate	E G A F P
Connectives effective	E G A F P

CONCLUSION

Prepared audience for ending	E G A F P
Reinforced central idea	E G A F P
Vivid ending	E G A F P

DELIVERY

Began speech without rushing	E G A F P
Maintained strong eye contact	E G A F P
Avoided distracting mannerisms	E G A F P
Articulated words clearly	E G A F P
Used pauses effectively	E G A F P
Used vocal variety to add impact	E G A F P
Prepared visual aids well	E G A F P
Presented visual aids well	E G A F P
Communicated enthusiasm for topic	E G A F P
Departed from lectern without rushing	E G A F P

OVERALL EVALUATION

Met assignment	E G A F P
Topic challenging	E G A F P
Specific purpose well chosen	E G A F P
Message adapted to audience	E G A F P
Speech completed within time limit	E G A F P
Held interest of audience	E G A F P

_____

What did the speaker do most effectively? _____

_____

_____

What should the speaker pay special attention to next time? _____

_____

_____

General Comments: _____

_____

_____

_____

SPEECH EVALUATION FORM

Speaker _____

Topic _____

Rate the speaker on each criteria: E-excellent G-good A-average F-fair P-poor

INTRODUCTION

Gained attention and interest — E G A F P
Introduced topic clearly — E G A F P
Related topic to audience — E G A F P
Established credibility — E G A F P
Previewed body of speech — E G A F P

BODY

Main points clear — E G A F P
Main points fully supported — E G A F P
Organization well planned — E G A F P
Language accurate — E G A F P
Language clear — E G A F P
Language appropriate — E G A F P
Connectives effective — E G A F P

CONCLUSION

Prepared audience for ending — E G A F P
Reinforced central idea — E G A F P
Vivid ending — E G A F P

DELIVERY

Began speech without rushing — E G A F P
Maintained strong eye contact — E G A F P
Avoided distracting mannerisms — E G A F P
Articulated words clearly — E G A F P
Used pauses effectively — E G A F P
Used vocal variety to add impact — E G A F P
Prepared visual aids well — E G A F P
Presented visual aids well — E G A F P
Communicated enthusiasm for topic — E G A F P
Departed from lectern without rushing — E G A F P

OVERALL EVALUATION

Met assignment — E G A F P
Topic challenging — E G A F P
Specific purpose well chosen — E G A F P
Message adapted to audience — E G A F P
Speech completed within time limit — E G A F P
Held interest of audience — E G A F P

What did the speaker do most effectively? _____

What should the speaker pay special attention to next time? _____

General Comments: _____

SPEECH EVALUATION FORM

Speaker _____

Topic _____

Rate the speaker on each point: *E-excellent*   *G-good*   *A-average*   *F-fair*   *P-poor*

INTRODUCTION

Gained attention and interest	E G A F P
Introduced topic clearly	E G A F P
Related topic to audience	E G A F P
Established credibility	E G A F P
Previewed body of speech	E G A F P

BODY

Main points clear	E G A F P
Main points fully supported	E G A F P
Organization well planned	E G A F P
Language accurate	E G A F P
Language clear	E G A F P
Language appropriate	E G A F P
Connectives effective	E G A F P

CONCLUSION

Prepared audience for ending	E G A F P
Reinforced central idea	E G A F P
Vivid ending	E G A F P

DELIVERY

Began speech without rushing	E G A F P
Maintained strong eye contact	E G A F P
Avoided distracting mannerisms	E G A F P
Articulated words clearly	E G A F P
Used pauses effectively	E G A F P
Used vocal variety to add impact	E G A F P
Prepared visual aids well	E G A F P
Presented visual aids well	E G A F P
Communicated enthusiasm for topic	E G A F P
Departed from lectern without rushing	E G A F P

OVERALL EVALUATION

Met assignment	E G A F P
Topic challenging	E G A F P
Specific purpose well chosen	E G A F P
Message adapted to audience	E G A F P
Speech completed within time limit	E G A F P
Held interest of audience	E G A F P

What did the speaker do most effectively? _____

_____

_____

What should the speaker pay special attention to next time? _____

_____

_____

General Comments: _____

_____

_____

_____

SPEECH EVALUATION FORM

Speaker _____

Topic _____

Rate the speaker on each point: Excellent   Good   Average   Fair   Poor

INTRODUCTION		DELIVERY	
Gained attention and interest	E G A F P	Began speech without rushing	E G A F P
Introduced topic clearly	E G A F P	Maintained strong eye contact	E G A F P
Related topic to audience	E G A F P	Avoided distracting mannerisms	E G A F P
Established credibility	E G A F P	Articulated words clearly	E G A F P
Previewed body of speech	E G A F P	Used pauses effectively	E G A F P
		Used vocal variety to add impact	E G A F P
BODY		Prepared visual aids well	E G A F P
Main points clear	E G A F P	Presented visual aids well	E G A F P
Main points fully supported	E G A F P	Communicated enthusiasm for topic	E G A F P
Organization well planned	E G A F P	Departed from lectern without rushing	E G A F P
Language accurate	E G A F P		
Language clear	E G A F P	OVERALL EVALUATION	
Language appropriate	E G A F P	Topic challenging	E G A F P
Connectives effective	E G A F P	Specific purpose clear	E G A F P
		Specific purpose worthwhile	E G A F P
CONCLUSION		Message adapted to audience	E G A F P
Prepared audience for ending	E G A F P	Speech completed within time limit	E G A F P
Reinforced central idea	E G A F P	Held interest of audience	E G A F P
Vivid ending	E G A F P		

What did the Speaker do most effectively?

_____

_____

What should the speaker pay special attention to next time?

_____

_____

General comments:

_____

_____

_____

SPEECH EVALUATION FORM

Speaker _____

Topic _____

Rate the speaker on each point: *E-excellent*   *G-good*   *A-average*   *F-fair*   *P-poor*

INTRODUCTION

Gained attention and interest	E G A F P
Introduced topic clearly	E G A F P
Related topic to audience	E G A F P
Established credibility	E G A F P
Previewed body of speech	E G A F P

BODY

Main points clear	E G A F P
Main points fully supported	E G A F P
Organization well planned	E G A F P
Language accurate	E G A F P
Language clear	E G A F P
Language appropriate	E G A F P
Connectives effective	E G A F P

CONCLUSION

Prepared audience for ending	E G A F P
Reinforced central idea	E G A F P
Vivid ending	E G A F P

DELIVERY

Began speech without rushing	E G A F P
Maintained strong eye contact	E G A F P
Avoided distracting mannerisms	E G A F P
Articulated words clearly	E G A F P
Used pauses effectively	E G A F P
Used vocal variety to add impact	E G A F P
Prepared visual aids well	E G A F P
Presented visual aids well	E G A F P
Communicated enthusiasm for topic	E G A F P
Departed from lectern without rushing	E G A F P

OVERALL EVALUATION

Met assignment	E G A F P
Topic challenging	E G A F P
Specific purpose well chosen	E G A F P
Message adapted to audience	E G A F P
Speech completed within time limit	E G A F P
Held interest of audience	E G A F P

_____

What did the speaker do most effectively? _____

_____

What should the speaker pay special attention to next time? _____

_____

_____

General Comments: _____

_____

_____

_____

SPEECH EVALUATION FORM

Speaker _____

Topic _____

Rate the speaker in each area: E-excellent   G-good   A-average   F-fair   P-poor

INTRODUCTION

Gained attention and interest	E G A F P
Introduced topic clearly	E G A F P
Related topic to audience	E G A F P
Established credibility	E G A F P
Previewed body of speech	E G A F P

BODY

Main points clear	E G A F P
Main points fully supported	E G A F P
Organization well planned	E G A F P
Language accurate	E G A F P
Language clear	E G A F P
Language appropriate	E G A F P
Connectives effective	E G A F P

CONCLUSION

Prepared audience for ending	E G A F P
Reinforced central idea	E G A F P
Vivid ending	E G A F P

DELIVERY

Began speech without rushing	E G A F P
Maintained strong eye contact	E G A F P
Avoided distracting mannerisms	E G A F P
Articulated words clearly	E G A F P
Used pauses effectively	E G A F P
Used vocal variety to add impact	E G A F P
Presented visual aids well	E G A F P
Communicated enthusiasm for topic	E G A F P
Departed from lectern without rushing	E G A F P

OVERALL EVALUATION

Met assignment	E G A F P
Topic challenging	E G A F P
Specific purpose well chosen	E G A F P
Message adapted to audience	E G A F P
Speech completed within time limit	E G A F P
Held interest of audience	E G A F P

What did the speaker do most effectively?

_____

_____

What should the speaker pay special attention to next time?

_____

_____

General Comment:

_____

_____

SPEECH EVALUATION FORM

Speaker _____

Topic _____

Rate the speaker on each point: *E-excellent*   *G-good*   *A-average*   *F-fair*   *P-poor*

INTRODUCTION

Gained attention and interest	E G A F P
Introduced topic clearly	E G A F P
Related topic to audience	E G A F P
Established credibility	E G A F P
Previewed body of speech	E G A F P

BODY

Main points clear	E G A F P
Main points fully supported	E G A F P
Organization well planned	E G A F P
Language accurate	E G A F P
Language clear	E G A F P
Language appropriate	E G A F P
Connectives effective	E G A F P

CONCLUSION

Prepared audience for ending	E G A F P
Reinforced central idea	E G A F P
Vivid ending	E G A F P

DELIVERY

Began speech without rushing	E G A F P
Maintained strong eye contact	E G A F P
Avoided distracting mannerisms	E G A F P
Articulated words clearly	E G A F P
Used pauses effectively	E G A F P
Used vocal variety to add impact	E G A F P
Prepared visual aids well	E G A F P
Presented visual aids well	E G A F P
Communicated enthusiasm for topic	E G A F P
Departed from lectern without rushing	E G A F P

OVERALL EVALUATION

Met assignment	E G A F P
Topic challenging	E G A F P
Specific purpose well chosen	E G A F P
Message adapted to audience	E G A F P
Speech completed within time limit	E G A F P
Held interest of audience	E G A F P

What did the speaker do most effectively? _____

_____

What should the speaker pay special attention to next time? _____

_____

General Comments: _____

_____

_____

SPEECH EVALUATION FORM

Speaker _____

Topic _____

Rate the Speaker on each point: Excellent   Good   Average   Fair   Poor

INTRODUCTION

Gained attention and interest   E G A F P
Introduced topic clearly   E G A F P
Related topic to audience   E G A F P
Established credibility   E G A F P
Previewed body of speech   E G A F P

BODY

Main points clear   E G A F P
Main points fully supported   E G A F P
Organization well planned   E G A F P
Language accurate   E G A F P
Language clear   E G A F P
Transitions appropriate   E G A F P
Connectives effective   E G A F P

CONCLUSION

Prepared audience for ending   E G A F P
Reinforced central idea   E G A F P
Vivid ending   E G A F P

DELIVERY

Began speech without rushing   E G A F P
Maintained eye contact   E G A F P
Avoided distracting mannerisms   E G A F P
Articulated words clearly   E G A F P
Used pauses effectively   E G A F P
Used vocal variety to add impact   E G A F P
Prepared visual aids well   E G A F P
Presented visual aids well   E G A F P
Communicated enthusiasm for topic   E G A F P
Departed from lectern without rushing   E G A F P

OVERALL EVALUATION

Met assignment   E G A F P
Topic challenging   E G A F P
Specific purpose well chosen   E G A F P
Message adapted to audience   E G A F P
Speech completed within time limit   E G A F P
Held interest of audience   E G A F P

What did the speaker do most effectively?

_____

_____

What should the speaker pay special attention to next time?

_____

_____

_____

General comments:

_____

_____

_____

SPEECH EVALUATION FORM

Speaker _____

Topic _____

Rate the speaker on each point: *E-excellent*   *G-good*   *A-average*   *F-fair*   *P-poor*

INTRODUCTION

Gained attention and interest	E G A F P
Introduced topic clearly	E G A F P
Related topic to audience	E G A F P
Established credibility	E G A F P
Previewed body of speech	E G A F P

BODY

Main points clear	E G A F P
Main points fully supported	E G A F P
Organization well planned	E G A F P
Language accurate	E G A F P
Language clear	E G A F P
Language appropriate	E G A F P
Connectives effective	E G A F P

CONCLUSION

Prepared audience for ending	E G A F P
Reinforced central idea	E G A F P
Vivid ending	E G A F P

DELIVERY

Began speech without rushing	E G A F P
Maintained strong eye contact	E G A F P
Avoided distracting mannerisms	E G A F P
Articulated words clearly	E G A F P
Used pauses effectively	E G A F P
Used vocal variety to add impact	E G A F P
Prepared visual aids well	E G A F P
Presented visual aids well	E G A F P
Communicated enthusiasm for topic	E G A F P
Departed from lectern without rushing	E G A F P

OVERALL EVALUATION

Met assignment	E G A F P
Topic challenging	E G A F P
Specific purpose well chosen	E G A F P
Message adapted to audience	E G A F P
Speech completed within time limit	E G A F P
Held interest of audience	E G A F P

_____

What did the speaker do most effectively? _____

_____

_____

What should the speaker pay special attention to next time? _____

_____

_____

General Comments: _____

_____

_____

_____

SPEECH EVALUATION FORM

Speaker _____

Topic _____

Rate the speaker on each point: E-excellent   G-good   A-average   F-fair   P-poor

INTRODUCTION

Gained attention and interest	E G A F P
Introduced topic clearly	E G A F P
Related topic to audience	E G A F P
Established credibility	E G A F P
Previewed body of speech	E G A F P

BODY

Main points clear	E G A F P
Main points fully supported	E G A F P
Organization well planned	E G A F P
Language accurate	E G A F P
Language clear	E G A F P
Language appropriate	E G A F P
Connectives effective	E G A F P

CONCLUSION

Prepared audience for ending	E G A F P
Reinforced central idea	E G A F P
Vivid ending	E G A F P

DELIVERY

Began speech without rushing	E G A F P
Maintained strong eye contact	E G A F P
Avoided distracting mannerisms	E G A F P
Articulated words clearly	E G A F P
Used pauses effectively	E G A F P
Used vocal variety to add impact	E G A F P
Prepared visual aids well	E G A F P
Presented visual aids well	E G A F P
Communicated enthusiasm for topic	E G A F P
Departed from lectern without rushing	E G A F P

OVERALL EVALUATION

Met assignment	E G A F P
Topic challenging	E G A F P
Specific purpose well chosen	E G A F P
Message adapted to audience	E G A F P
Speech completed within time limit	E G A F P
Held interest of audience	E G A F P

What did the speaker do most effectively?

_____

_____

_____

What should the speaker pay special attention to next time?

_____

_____

_____

General Comments:

_____

_____

_____

SPEECH EVALUATION FORM

Speaker _____

Topic _____

Rate the speaker on each point: *E-excellent*   *G-good*   *A-average*   *F-fair*   *P-poor*

INTRODUCTION

Gained attention and interest	E G A F P
Introduced topic clearly	E G A F P
Related topic to audience	E G A F P
Established credibility	E G A F P
Previewed body of speech	E G A F P

BODY

Main points clear	E G A F P
Main points fully supported	E G A F P
Organization well planned	E G A F P
Language accurate	E G A F P
Language clear	E G A F P
Language appropriate	E G A F P
Connectives effective	E G A F P

CONCLUSION

Prepared audience for ending	E G A F P
Reinforced central idea	E G A F P
Vivid ending	E G A F P

DELIVERY

Began speech without rushing	E G A F P
Maintained strong eye contact	E G A F P
Avoided distracting mannerisms	E G A F P
Articulated words clearly	E G A F P
Used pauses effectively	E G A F P
Used vocal variety to add impact	E G A F P
Prepared visual aids well	E G A F P
Presented visual aids well	E G A F P
Communicated enthusiasm for topic	E G A F P
Departed from lectern without rushing	E G A F P

OVERALL EVALUATION

Met assignment	E G A F P
Topic challenging	E G A F P
Specific purpose well chosen	E G A F P
Message adapted to audience	E G A F P
Speech completed within time limit	E G A F P
Held interest of audience	E G A F P

_____

What did the speaker do most effectively? _____

_____

What should the speaker pay special attention to next time? _____

_____

_____

General Comments: _____

_____

_____

_____

SPEECH EVALUATION FORM

Speaker:

Topic:

Rate the speaker on each 5-point scale: Excellent   Very good   Average   Fair   Poor

INTRODUCTION

Gained attention and interest	E	G	A	F	P
Introduced topic clearly	E	G	A	F	P
Related topic to audience	E	G	A	F	P
Established credibility	E	G	A	F	P
Previewed body of speech	E	G	A	F	P

BODY

Main points clear	E	G	A	F	P
Main points fully supported	E	G	A	F	P
Organization well planned	E	G	A	F	P
Language accurate	E	G	A	F	P
Language clear	E	G	A	F	P
Language appropriate	E	G	A	F	P
Connectives effective	E	G	A	F	P

CONCLUSION

Prepared audience for ending	E	G	A	F	P
Reinforced central idea	E	G	A	F	P
Vivid ending	E	G	A	F	P

DELIVERY

Began speech without rushing	E	G	A	F	P
Maintained strong eye contact	E	G	A	F	P
Avoided distracting mannerisms	E	G	A	F	P
Articulated words clearly	E	G	A	F	P
Used pauses effectively	E	G	A	F	P
Used vocal variety to add impact	E	G	A	F	P
Prepared visual aids well	E	G	A	F	P
Presented visual aids well	E	G	A	F	P
Communicated enthusiasm for topic	E	G	A	F	P
Departed from lectern without rushing	E	G	A	F	P

OVERALL EVALUATION

Met assignment	E	G	A	F	P
Topic challenging	E	G	A	F	P
Specific purpose well chosen	E	G	A	F	P
Message adapted to audience	E	G	A	F	P
Speech completed within time limit	E	G	A	F	P
Held interest of audience	E	G	A	F	P

What did the speaker do most effectively?

What should the speaker pay special attention to next time?

General comments:

SPEECH EVALUATION FORM

Speaker _____

Topic _____

Rate the speaker on each point: *E-excellent*   *G-good*   *A-average*   *F-fair*   *P-poor*

INTRODUCTION

Gained attention and interest	E G A F P
Introduced topic clearly	E G A F P
Related topic to audience	E G A F P
Established credibility	E G A F P
Previewed body of speech	E G A F P

BODY

Main points clear	E G A F P
Main points fully supported	E G A F P
Organization well planned	E G A F P
Language accurate	E G A F P
Language clear	E G A F P
Language appropriate	E G A F P
Connectives effective	E G A F P

CONCLUSION

Prepared audience for ending	E G A F P
Reinforced central idea	E G A F P
Vivid ending	E G A F P

DELIVERY

Began speech without rushing	E G A F P
Maintained strong eye contact	E G A F P
Avoided distracting mannerisms	E G A F P
Articulated words clearly	E G A F P
Used pauses effectively	E G A F P
Used vocal variety to add impact	E G A F P
Prepared visual aids well	E G A F P
Presented visual aids well	E G A F P
Communicated enthusiasm for topic	E G A F P
Departed from lectern without rushing	E G A F P

OVERALL EVALUATION

Met assignment	E G A F P
Topic challenging	E G A F P
Specific purpose well chosen	E G A F P
Message adapted to audience	E G A F P
Speech completed within time limit	E G A F P
Held interest of audience	E G A F P

_____

What did the speaker do most effectively? _____

_____

What should the speaker pay special attention to next time? _____

_____

General Comments: _____

_____

_____

_____

SPEECH EVALUATION FORM

Speaker _____

Topic _____

Rate the speaker on each item: E = excellent   G = good   A = average   F = fair   P = poor

INTRODUCTION

Gained attention and interest	E G A F P
Introduced topic clearly	E G A F P
Related topic to audience	E G A F P
Established credibility	E G A F P
Previewed body of speech	E G A F P

BODY

Main points clear	E G A F P
Main points fully supported	E G A F P
Organization well planned	E G A F P
Language accurate	E G A F P
Language clear	E G A F P
Language appropriate	E G A F P
Connectives effective	E G A F P

CONCLUSION

Prepared audience for ending	E G A F P
Reinforced central idea	E G A F P
Vivid ending	E G A F P

DELIVERY

Began speech without rushing	E G A F P
Maintained strong eye contact	E G A F P
Avoided distracting mannerisms	E G A F P
Articulated words clearly	E G A F P
Used pauses effectively	E G A F P
Used vocal variety to add impact	E G A F P
Prepared visual aids well	E G A F P
Presented visual aids well	E G A F P
Communicated enthusiasm for topic	E G A F P
Departed from lectern without rushing	E G A F P

OVERALL EVALUATION

Met assignment	E G A F P
Topic challenging	E G A F P
Specific purpose well chosen	E G A F P
Message adapted to audience	E G A F P
Speech completed within time limit	E G A F P
Held interest of audience	E G A F P

What did the speaker do most effectively?

_____

What should the speaker pay special attention to next time?

_____

General Comments:

_____

SPEECH EVALUATION FORM

Speaker _____

Topic _____

Rate the speaker on each point: *E-excellent*   *G-good*   *A-average*   *F-fair*   *P-poor*

INTRODUCTION

Gained attention and interest	E G A F P
Introduced topic clearly	E G A F P
Related topic to audience	E G A F P
Established credibility	E G A F P
Previewed body of speech	E G A F P

BODY

Main points clear	E G A F P
Main points fully supported	E G A F P
Organization well planned	E G A F P
Language accurate	E G A F P
Language clear	E G A F P
Language appropriate	E G A F P
Connectives effective	E G A F P

CONCLUSION

Prepared audience for ending	E G A F P
Reinforced central idea	E G A F P
Vivid ending	E G A F P

DELIVERY

Began speech without rushing	E G A F P
Maintained strong eye contact	E G A F P
Avoided distracting mannerisms	E G A F P
Articulated words clearly	E G A F P
Used pauses effectively	E G A F P
Used vocal variety to add impact	E G A F P
Prepared visual aids well	E G A F P
Presented visual aids well	E G A F P
Communicated enthusiasm for topic	E G A F P
Departed from lectern without rushing	E G A F P

OVERALL EVALUATION

Met assignment	E G A F P
Topic challenging	E G A F P
Specific purpose well chosen	E G A F P
Message adapted to audience	E G A F P
Speech completed within time limit	E G A F P
Held interest of audience	E G A F P

_____

What did the speaker do most effectively? _____

_____

What should the speaker pay special attention to next time? _____

_____

_____

General Comments: _____

_____

_____

_____

SPEECH EVALUATION FORM

Speaker _____

Topic _____

Rate the speaker on each point: *E-excellent*   *G-good*   *A-average*   *F-fair*   *P-poor*

INTRODUCTION

Gained attention and interest	E G A F P
Introduced topic clearly	E G A F P
Related topic to audience	E G A F P
Established credibility	E G A F P
Previewed body of speech	E G A F P

BODY

Main points clear	E G A F P
Main points fully supported	E G A F P
Organization well planned	E G A F P
Language accurate	E G A F P
Language clear	E G A F P
Language appropriate	E G A F P
Connectives effective	E G A F P

CONCLUSION

Prepared audience for ending	E G A F P
Reinforced central idea	E G A F P
Vivid ending	E G A F P

DELIVERY

Began speech without rushing	E G A F P
Maintained strong eye contact	E G A F P
Avoided distracting mannerisms	E G A F P
Articulated words clearly	E G A F P
Used pauses effectively	E G A F P
Used vocal variety to add impact	E G A F P
Prepared visual aids well	E G A F P
Presented visual aids well	E G A F P
Communicated enthusiasm for topic	E G A F P
Departed from lectern without rushing	E G A F P

OVERALL EVALUATION

Met assignment	E G A F P
Topic challenging	E G A F P
Specific purpose well chosen	E G A F P
Message adapted to audience	E G A F P
Speech completed within time limit	E G A F P
Held interest of audience	E G A F P

_____

What did the speaker do most effectively? _____

_____

_____

What should the speaker pay special attention to next time? _____

_____

_____

General Comments: _____

_____

_____

_____

SPEECH EVALUATION FORM

Speaker _____

Topic _____

Rate the speaker on each point.   E=excellent   G=good   A=average   F=fair   P=poor

INTRODUCTION

Gained attention and interest   E G A F P
Introduced topic clearly   E G A F P
Related topic to audience   E G A F P
Established credibility   E G A F P
Previewed body of speech   E G A F P

BODY

Main points clear   E G A F P
Main points fully supported   E G A F P
Organization well planned   E G A F P
Language accurate   E G A F P
Language clear   E G A F P
Language appropriate   E G A F P
Connectives effective   E G A F P

CONCLUSION

Prepared audience for ending   E G A F P
Reinforced central idea   E G A F P
Vivid ending   E G A F P

DELIVERY

Began speech without rushing   E G A F P
Maintained strong eye contact   E G A F P
Avoided distracting mannerisms   E G A F P
Articulated words clearly   E G A F P
Used pauses effectively   E G A F P
Used vocal variety to add impact   E G A F P
Prepared visual aids well   E G A F P
Presented visual aids well   E G A F P
Communicated enthusiasm for topic   E G A F P
Departed from lectern without rushing E G A F P

OVERALL EVALUATION

Met assignment   E G A F P
Topic challenging   E G A F P
Specific purpose well chosen   E G A F P
Message adapted to audience   E G A F P
Speech completed within time limit   E G A F P
Held interest of audience   E G A F P

What did the speaker do most effectively?
_____
_____

What should the speaker pay special attention to next time?
_____
_____

General Comments:
_____
_____

SPEECH EVALUATION FORM

Speaker _____

Topic _____

Rate the speaker on each point: *E-excellent   G-good   A-average   F-fair   P-poor*

INTRODUCTION

Gained attention and interest	E G A F P
Introduced topic clearly	E G A F P
Related topic to audience	E G A F P
Established credibility	E G A F P
Previewed body of speech	E G A F P

BODY

Main points clear	E G A F P
Main points fully supported	E G A F P
Organization well planned	E G A F P
Language accurate	E G A F P
Language clear	E G A F P
Language appropriate	E G A F P
Connectives effective	E G A F P

CONCLUSION

Prepared audience for ending	E G A F P
Reinforced central idea	E G A F P
Vivid ending	E G A F P

DELIVERY

Began speech without rushing	E G A F P
Maintained strong eye contact	E G A F P
Avoided distracting mannerisms	E G A F P
Articulated words clearly	E G A F P
Used pauses effectively	E G A F P
Used vocal variety to add impact	E G A F P
Prepared visual aids well	E G A F P
Presented visual aids well	E G A F P
Communicated enthusiasm for topic	E G A F P
Departed from lectern without rushing	E G A F P

OVERALL EVALUATION

Met assignment	E G A F P
Topic challenging	E G A F P
Specific purpose well chosen	E G A F P
Message adapted to audience	E G A F P
Speech completed within time limit	E G A F P
Held interest of audience	E G A F P

_____

What did the speaker do most effectively? _____

_____

_____

What should the speaker pay special attention to next time? _____

_____

_____

General Comments: _____

_____

_____

_____

SPEECH EVALUATION FORM

Speaker _____

Topic _____

Rate the speaker on each point: E-excellent   G-good   A-average   F-fair   P-poor

INTRODUCTION

Gained attention and interest	E G A F P
Introduced topic clearly	E G A F P
Related topic to audience	E G A F P
Established credibility	E G A F P
Previewed body of speech	E G A F P

BODY

Main points clear	E G A F P
Main points fully supported	E G A F P
Organization well planned	E G A F P
Language accurate	E G A F P
Language clear	E G A F P
Language appropriate	E G A F P
Connectives effective	E G A F P

CONCLUSION

Prepared audience for ending	E G A F P
Reinforced central idea	E G A F P
Vivid ending	E G A F P

DELIVERY

Began speech without rushing	E G A F P
Maintained eye contact	E G A F P
Avoided distracting mannerisms	E G A F P
Articulation clear	E G A F P
Used pauses effectively	E G A F P
Used voice to add impact	E G A F P
Regulated voice effectively	E G A F P
Presented visual aids well	E G A F P
Gestures and facial expression effective	E G A F P
Departed from lectern without rushing	E G A F P

OVERALL EVALUATION

Met assignment	E G A F P
Topic challenging	E G A F P
Specific purpose well chosen	E G A F P
Message adapted to audience	E G A F P
Speech completed within time limit	E G A F P
Held interest of audience	E G A F P

What did the speaker do most effectively? _____

What should the speaker give special attention to next time? _____

General Comments _____